Heinemann **Scottish** History | S.A.T.H.

Renaissance, Reformation
AND THE Age of Discovery
1700

o

Tom Monaghan

Series editor: Jim McGonigle

Heinemann Educational Publishers
Halley Court, Jordan Hill, Oxford, OX2 8EJ
a division of Reed Educational & Professional Publishing Ltd

Heinemann is a registered trademark of Reed Educational & Professional Publishing Ltd

OXFORD MELBOURNE AUCKLAND
JOHANNESBURG BLANTYRE GABORONE
IBADAN PORTSMOUTH NH (USA) CHICAGO

© Tom Monaghan 2002

First published 2002

ISBN 0 435 32090 4
04 03 02
10 9 8 7 6 5 4 3 2 1

941.105

ABS2049930

Designed and typeset by Ken Vail Graphic Design, Cambridge

Printed and bound in the United Kingdom by Bath Colour books

Picture research by Jenny Silkstone

Photographic acknowledgements
The author and publisher would like to thank the following for permission to
reproduce photographs:
AKG London: 34; Ashmoleum Museum: 42 (top); Bridgeman Art Library: 10, 41; Bridgeman
Art Library/Galleria degli Uffizi, Florence, Italy: 32; Bridgeman Art Library/National Museums
of Scotland: 49; Bridgeman Art Library/Philip Mould, Historical Portraits Ltd: 28, 57; Bridgeman
Art Library/Scottish National Portrait Gallery, Edinburgh: 4; Bridgeman Art Library/Trustees of
the Weston Park Foundation: 39; The Burrell Collection/Glasgow Museums: Art Gallery &
Museum, Kelvingrove: 51; Historical Archive: 13, 27, 29, 36 (top right); Mary Evans Picture
Library: 19, 21, 47; MSS National Library of Scotland: 60; National Portrait Gallery:
42 (bottom), 46; Osterreichische National Bibliothek: 7; Royal Bank of Scotland plc: 55;
SCRAN/Edinburgh College of Art: 25; SCRAN/National Museums of Scotland: 36 (top left);
SCRAN/Scotsman Publications: 17; St Andrews University Library, Photographic Collection:
36 (bottom); Trustees of the National Museums of Scotland: 9, 44

Cover photograph: © Bridgeman Art Library/Phillips. The painting is
'Mary Stuart's Farewell to France' by Henry Nelson O'Neil, 1862.

Written sources acknowledgements
The author and the publishers gratefully acknowledge the following
publications from which written sources in the book are drawn. In some
sources the wording or sentence structure has been simplified.

G. Menzies, *In Search of Scotland* (Polygon/Edinburgh University Press, 2001): 24A
C. Tabraham & D. Grove, *Fortress Scotland and the Jacobites* (B.T. Batsford/Historic
Scotland, 1995): 42C

Contents

James IV succeeds his father

On 11 June 1488, an army of Scottish rebels, led by Prince James, fought King James III's army at Sauchieburn. The king's troops were defeated. As the king tried to escape from the battlefield, he was thrown from his horse and murdered as he lay injured in the mill at Bannockburn. Two weeks later, on 25 June 1488, the young prince was crowned King James IV at Scone. It is said that the new King of Scots wore a heavy belt with iron weights hanging from it as a punishment for the circumstances of his father's death.

Why was there a rebellion?

The rebel nobles hoped that they could rule as regents to the young prince, once they had captured King James III. They planned to use young James as a figurehead, since he was still a teenager. The prince agreed to lead the rebels, so long as no harm came to his father.

Faced with this challenge to his power, King James III found that few of the nobles who supported him wanted to join his army in order to fight the rebels. Instead, most nobles chose to wait and see who would win: the king or his eldest son and heir? The loyalty of Scotland's nobles towards their monarch would be called into question many times over the next two centuries.

The Lord of the Isles

The new king, James IV, quickly made it clear that he did not intend to share his power with anyone, including the leading rebel families, the Homes and Hepburns.

However, in the Scottish Highlands and Islands, John, Chief of Clan Donald, ruled as Lord of the Isles and it was his word that was obeyed there, rather than the king's. In 1493, James IV ordered John to give up his titles and lands and, although John agreed, James had to lead several attacks against Clan Donald and its supporters because they refused to obey him.

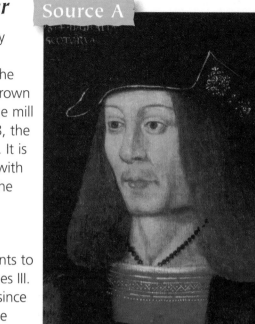

▲ *King James IV of Scotland, painted in 1491.*

The Highland Clans

The gaelic-speaking clans lived in the Scottish Highlands and Western Isles. They were led by chiefs who had as much power over their clanspeople as a king or queen. The people of the clan lived on the chief's land, and they paid their rent to the chief, or to one of his relatives or friends. Clansmen had to fight for their chief when asked, and the larger, more powerful clans fought each other over family disputes, and for land and cattle. Outside the Lowlands of Scotland, the King of Scots had little control over the clan chiefs.

Seven years later, James made the Chief of Clan Campbell his Lieutenant, or representative, in the lands taken from Clan Donald. The following year, James gave the Gordons similar power in the north-east of Scotland. He hoped that these two families would help him to restore respect for royal authority in the Highlands. Despite these efforts to bring peace and order to the Highlands, the grandson of John, Chief of Clan Donald, tried to regain his grandfather's title of Lord of the Isles in 1504.

Some historians say that James did not succeed in bringing the Highlands under royal control. Instead, he gave too much power to the Campbells and Gordons. These families were loyal to the king, but often stirred up trouble between themselves.

Scotland, France and England

James IV was in contact with monarchs in other countries. He improved relations with France, and he signed the Treaty of Perpetual Peace with England in 1502, which stated that England and Scotland would no longer go to war with each other. The next year, James married Margaret Tudor, a daughter of Henry VII, King of England. This marriage would make possible the Union of the Crowns between the two countries a century later. In the short term, however, James could not be friends with both England and France, who were traditional enemies. Reviving the Auld Alliance with France thus brought the treaty with England to a swift end: the Auld Alliance refers to the agreement that Scotland would join with France in any dispute with England and vice versa. This would lead to war between James IV and his brother-in-law, Henry VIII, and the Scottish king's death in battle.

> ## Questions
>
> 1. To what extent could James IV be held responsible for his father's death?
>
> 2. Why did James IV set out to reduce the power of the Lord of the Isles?
>
> 3. In what ways did James IV attempt to bring Scotland and England closer together?

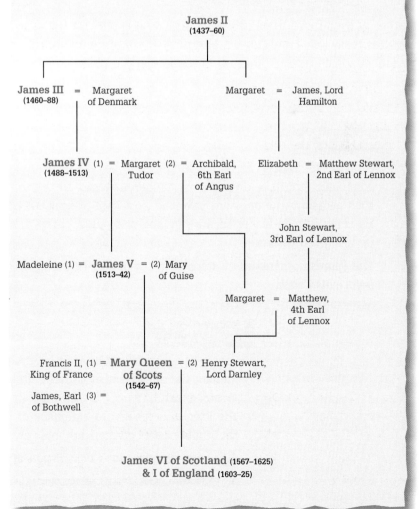

The Stewart family tree to 1625.

Historical enquiry – What was James IV really like?

James IV (1473–1513) is one of the most significant figures in Scottish history. His efforts to encourage learning, and his attempts to unite his kingdom by destroying the power of the Lord of the Isles, made him an important influence on the rest of the sixteenth century.

James IV wanted to be seen as a 'renaissance king'. The Renaissance of the fourteenth and fifteenth centuries was a time of a 'rebirth' of knowledge and culture in Europe. Artists, architects, teachers, scientists and writers rediscovered the ideas of Ancient Greece and Rome. Kings and princes encouraged the spread of these ideas, James amongst them. For example, James financed the completion of the magnificent Great Hall at Stirling Castle, and allowed Walter Chapman and Andrew Myllar to set up the first printing press in Scotland, which meant that books could be produced more quickly and cheaply than before. The printers published the Acts of the Scottish Parliament, and other notable books, though they made more money from printing books of poetry by people such as William Dunbar and Robert Henryson than printing law books.

James IV lived more than 500 years ago, so it is difficult for us to know what he was really like. How can we find out? There are many different types of evidence which give us clues about people in the past.

6

- *Written evidence*, from records of what people said about James IV.

Source B

He is brave, even more than a king should be ... I have often seen him take on the most dangerous tasks. On such occasions, he does not take the least care of himself. He is not a good leader because he begins to fight before he has given his orders.

The Spanish ambassador's description of James IV shortly before his death.

Source C

James IV speaks the following languages: Latin, very well, French, German, Flemish (Dutch), Italian and Spanish ... his own Scottish language is quite different from that of England. The king also speaks the language of the natives who live in the remote parts of the Highlands and Islands (Gaelic).

A foreign ambassador's description of the young Scottish king.

● *Visual evidence*, such as portraits.

Source D

James IV in full state dress of cloth of gold, kneeling at prayer. His patron saint, St James, stands behind him.

● What James IV is reported to have done.

● Information contained in old documents, such as wardrobe and laundry lists.

Source E

His subjects serve him with their persons and their goods, in just and unjust quarrels, exactly as he likes, and that therefore he does not think it right to begin any warlike undertaking without himself being the first in danger.

A foreign ambassador's note of a conversation that he had with James IV shortly before his death.

Source F

In 1490, the king owned 32 gowns, 47 doublets, 5 jackets, 2 hawking coats, 7 cloaks, 35 bonnets, 15 hats and 64 pairs of stockings.

Fashion among royalty and nobles in the early sixteenth century meant that James IV would wear a long gown when at home, and a short, padded or fur-lined jacket called a doublet when he was travelling. When hunting, he would wear a hawking coat, and most portraits show the king wearing a hat or crown.

Questions

1. Why do you think historians have to be careful about believing what we see in the portraits, such as Source D?

2. What evidence in Source F convinces you that James took a great pride in his appearance?

3. After looking at Sources B–F, what would you say if someone asked you, 'What was James IV really like?'

Death and defeat at the Battle of Flodden, 1513

In 1513, Henry VIII of England and Louis XII of France were at war over disputed territory. That summer, James IV decided to support the French king and honour the Auld Alliance, so he went to war against England. In return for James's support against England, Louis XII promised to support the Scottish king's ambitious plan to lead a crusade (a holy war) against the Muslim Ottoman, or Turkish, Empire, which controlled Jerusalem and the Holy Land. James was also angry at the loss of two Scottish ships, and the death of one of his admirals at the hands of the English navy.

The crusades

For several hundred years, Christians and Muslims had been fighting wars over territory. Christian monarchs such as Richard the Lionheart of England had fought long and hard to take control of Jerusalem away from the Muslims. The people of both religions regarded that city as being important to their religion. Since these wars were fought for religious reasons, they were called 'crusades' or holy wars. By the fifteenth century, most European kings and queens realised that the expense and danger of going on crusade made such expeditions impractical.

The battle

In August 1513 the Scottish army marched south from Edinburgh. By 9 September it had taken up its position at the top of Flodden Hill. This was a good position, but the English army marched across the River Till and moved into position behind the Scots, so that the Scots were forced to move to Branxton Hill. The Scottish cannon at the top of the hill were large, but they were difficult to aim, slow to reload, and not very accurate. The English cannon, with their expert gunners, were very effective, and forced the Scots to flee their defensive position at the top of the hill.

There were roughly 20,000 troops on both sides, but the best of the Scottish artillery had sailed with the Scottish navy to try to attack the English coast. This meant that the Scots' only remaining option was to charge the English army. In the hand-to-hand fighting that followed, the Scots were heavily defeated. The Scots' five-metre-long spears were no match for the shorter English bills or halberds (axe-like weapons – see Source G on page 9) that could chop off the Scottish spear-points. James IV, one of his sons, the Archbishop of St Andrews, three Highland chiefs, many earls and other nobles, and nearly 12,000 Scottish soldiers, were killed. James's body was not identified, and most of the dead were buried in huge pits that were dug after the battle.

━━━ *What were the results of the battle?*

A few months after James IV had been killed at the Battle of Flodden, the French made peace with the English, without even consulting the Scots. At that time, peace with England was more important to the French than their alliance with the Scots. This was because the powerful Hapsburg Empire, which controlled the Netherlands and Spain, close to France, was a greater threat than England. This meant that the French needed to concentrate on what was happening in Europe, and not concern itself with war against England.

After James IV's death, in the following reigns of James V and Mary Queen of Scots, Scottish nobles would disagree over whether they should be pro-English or pro-French.

A sixteenth-century halberd. ▶

Source G

9

Questions

1. What reasons can you find for James IV to declare war on England?

2. Was James IV brave or foolish to have led his army into battle? Discuss.

Extension task

1. Do you think the Scots should have been pro-French or pro-English in the sixteenth century?

Give at least two reasons for your answer.

Henry VIII: divorce and reform of the English church

From divorce to Reformation

Henry VIII ruled England from 1509 to 1547. Scotland's relations with England during the reign of Henry VIII played a large part in the political and religious history of Scotland.

In the 1520s Henry decided to divorce his wife, Catherine of Aragon, and marry Anne Boleyn, as Catherine had failed to produce a male heir. Royalty and nobility could be granted divorces or annulments by the Pope. However, Pope Clement VII was not willing to grant Henry a divorce from Catherine because she was the aunt of Charles V, ruler of the powerful Hapsburg Empire which controlled part of Italy, and the Pope did not want to anger Charles. As a result, Henry decided to take personal control of the church in England, in place of the Pope in Rome. This was a political decision, but it would lead to religious reform in the English church.

Source A

Henry VIII, a later portrait.

A Protestant church in England

Henry VIII called for a parliament to meet and pass a series of laws that made the English monarch Supreme Head of the Church of England. This parliament became known as the Reformation Parliament. Although there were few Protestants in England at that time, the result of these changes was that the Church of England became a Protestant church.

The presence of a Protestant state in England encouraged many Scots to discuss whether or not the church in Scotland should remain Catholic. James V was unwilling to reform the Scottish church. Also, he resisted Henry VIII's attempts to break the Auld Alliance between Scotland and France, which had been strengthened by the marriage of James V to Mary of Guise in 1538 (see family tree on page 5). Mary was French, and belonged to a family that was strongly opposed to Protestant ideas.

Relations between Scotland and Henry VIII broke down completely in 1542 when a Scottish army invaded England in revenge for an English attack on the south of Scotland, and was defeated at Solway Moss. James V died three weeks after this defeat. He was succeeded by his baby daughter, Mary Queen of Scots, with her mother – Mary of Guise – as regent. Although Mary Queen of Scots was Catholic, the Scottish church became a Protestant church during her reign, despite the protests of Catholics in Scotland and France.

Mary of Guise

On 1 January 1537, James V married Madeleine, the daughter of Francis I, King of France, at Notre Dame Cathedral in Paris. Sadly, Madeleine died in July 1537, weeks after arriving in Scotland. Within a year, James had married a second French bride. His new wife was Mary of Guise, who was 22-years-old and was a widow. Henry VIII described Mary as of 'majestic stature and graceful proportions'. Mary and James V had two sons, James and Arthur, but both had died by 1541. In December 1542, Mary of Guise gave birth to a daughter who was christened Mary, less than a week before her father, James V, died.

11

Questions

1. Why did Pope Clement VII refuse to grant Henry VIII his divorce?

2. What significance did the marriage of James V to Mary of Guise have for Henry VIII?

The church in sixteenth-century Scotland

The church in sixteenth-century Scotland was run by two archbishops and thirteen bishops. The Archbishop of St Andrews was the most senior of these church leaders. The bishops were in charge of large areas of land called dioceses, and each diocese was divided into parishes that were looked after by priests. Scotland also had a large number of other religious communities called monasteries, priories, friaries and convents, where monks, friars and nuns lived, prayed and worked. Bishops, priests and members of the religious communities did not pay the same taxes as other Scots, and they had their own law courts.

The Scottish church was a very wealthy organisation. Over the centuries, many rich Scots had given land to the church, and the archbishops, bishops and other important church leaders collected rents from this property. The church also collected a special tax from those who attended church, and even poor Scots were expected to donate gifts to the church on a regular basis. It was estimated that the Church of Scotland had an annual income that was twenty times greater than that of the king or queen. To take advantage of this wealth, and limit the power of the church, the Stewart dynasty always made sure that relatives and noble friends were appointed to important positions within the church.

How did the Stewarts make use of the church?

In 1532, the twenty-year-old King James V had obtained permission to appoint family members as abbots and priors of wealthy religious communities in Kelso, St Andrews, Pittenweem, Holyrood, Coldingham and Charterhouse. Criticisms of the corruption of the Church of Scotland were often linked with criticisms of the Stewarts, and the way that the royal family took advantage of the wealth of the church for their own benefit. In this way, the future of the Catholic Church in Scotland was linked to the fortunes of the Stewart dynasty. Any weaknesses shown by the royal family were to have serious repercussions for the Scottish church, at a time when people throughout western Europe were demanding reform of the Catholic Church.

Source B

◀ *Portrait of James V of Scotland, 1512–42.*

Reformation in Scotland

At the beginning of the sixteenth century, Christians in western Europe who wanted to see changes to the way that the Catholic Church was organised became known as Protestants. In many countries, religious wars broke out between Catholics, who were loyal to the existing church, and the Protestant reformers who wanted to break the power of the bishops and archbishops, including the Pope (who was bishop of Rome), and introduce many changes to the existing church.

For centuries, Scottish politics had been dominated by relations with France and England. During the Reformation, France remained a Catholic country, while England became Protestant. In the 1540s, as Scottish nobles who were either pro-French or pro-English struggled to gain control of the Scottish government, Scottish Protestants looked to England for support in their struggle to reform the church in Scotland. Scottish Protestants smuggled English translations of the Bible, translated from Latin, into Scotland.

As in many European countries, the future of the Protestant Church in Scotland was linked to political events. Events during the reign of Mary Queen of Scots, when her mother, Mary of Guise, was regent, meant that the Church of Scotland became a Protestant church, rather than remain Catholic. Hostility to Catholic Mary of Guise and her French advisers had encouraged opponents to look to Protestant England for advice and military support.

Some German states, and all of Scandinavia, adopted the Protestant ideas of the reformer Martin Luther. In other German states, the Netherlands, Switzerland and parts of France, Protestant reformers supported the ideas of John Calvin, who was based in Geneva in Switzerland. Many influential Protestant preachers in Scotland, such as John Knox, became Calvinists during the Reformation. However, political developments in Scotland during the reigns of Mary Queen of Scots, and her son, James VI, meant that the Protestant Church in Scotland was neither Lutheran nor Calvinist at the end of the sixteenth century. The basic principles of the Church of Scotland would not be agreed and confirmed until the end of the seventeenth century.

13

John Knox: voice of the people?

Source C

John Knox was a Catholic priest who was attracted to the ideas of the Protestant preacher George Wishart. In 1546, Scotland's Catholic bishops, led by Cardinal Beaton, ordered Wishart to be burned at the stake in St Andrews for preaching Protestant ideas. Later, Knox supported the murderers of Cardinal Beaton (see page 15), but the murderers were captured and executed and Knox was sentenced to forced labour on a French galley. When he was set free three years later, Knox made a name for himself as a Protestant preacher in England. Knox then fled to Geneva in Switzerland when Henry VIII's Catholic daughter, Mary Tudor, became queen in 1553.

Portrait of John Knox, whose sermon ▶
in St John's Kirk in Perth caused a riot.

Knox and Protestant ideas about church reform

In England and Geneva, Knox developed his ideas about how best to reform the Church of Scotland. He was influenced by European reformers such as John Calvin (1509–64), but for most Scots, whose religious education was limited, Knox set out his ideas in a clear and straightforward manner.

- He hated the wealth of the clergy in the Catholic Church, and he saw no need for cardinals, archbishops or bishops.
- He was against the use of Latin in church services and believed that the Bible should be made available to the Scots in their own language.
- He wanted to clear churches of statues and other 'Catholic' decorations, and argued that places of worship should be plain and simple.
- He believed that priests should be replaced by preachers, or ministers, who were chosen by each congregation.
- Above all, the Church of Scotland should be free to manage its own affairs, without interference from the royal family or its regents.

Knox briefly returned to Scotland in 1555, where his preaching and ideas about reforming the church in Scotland impressed the nobles and lairds who would form the influential Lords of the Faithful Congregation (see page 18). Knox then settled in Scotland in 1559. That same year, at St John's Kirk in Perth, he preached a sermon about his desire to see the Scottish church reformed as soon as possible. The sermon sparked off a riot that led to the destruction of Catholic statues and other images in the burgh's many churches and religious communities.

The 'monstrous regiment of women'!

In the 1560s, Knox was the minister of Edinburgh, and led the opposition to the religious policies of Mary Queen of Scots. For example, he wrote *First Blast of the Trumpet against the Monstrous Regiment of Women* as an attack on female rulers. Knox and his supporters wrote the first *Book of Discipline* that they claimed would provide a blueprint for a Protestant Church of Scotland, but this book was largely ignored by Scotland's Reformation Parliament. Knox died in 1572.

Questions

1. Why was the Church of Scotland so wealthy?

2. Why were the Stewarts accused of taking advantage of the Catholic Church in Scotland?

3. How did the Reformation in England help Scottish Protestants?

4. When Mary of Guise was regent, do you think that Scottish Protestants were pro-French or pro-English?

14

The 'rough wooing'

At Greenwich in 1543, Henry VIII of England tried to force the Scots into accepting that Mary Queen of Scots should marry Henry's son and heir, Edward. The Scots called this the 'rough wooing' as it was a brutal attempt to push the Scots into allowing their queen to marry the English prince. The marriage was intended to unite the two royal families of England and Scotland and therefore lead to the eventual union of both kingdoms.

In 1544, those Scots who were loyal to their young queen refused to accept the terms of the Treaty of Greenwich (see Source D). Angered by this, Henry VIII sent an English army, led by the Earl of Hertford, to invade Scotland. The invading Protestant army took control of Edinburgh and seized property from Scottish churches, monasteries and other religious communities. In 1545, the Scottish army defeated their English opponents at the battle of Ancrum Moor. However, the English invaders returned to burn crops and steal more property later that year. With a little effort, the Scottish army could defeat the English invaders. However, demands for religious reform by a growing number of Scottish Protestants could not be silenced as easily.

Source D

We have agreed ... that ... Prince Edward, eldest son and nearest apparent and undoubted heir of the unconquered and most powerful Prince Henry VIII, by Grace of God, King of England, France and Ireland ... as yet of less age and not six years old, shall marry ... Mary Queen of Scots ... not yet out of her first year.

Extract from the Treaty of Greenwich, 1543.

Cardinal Beaton, who was Archbishop of St Andrews, was unpopular with many Scots because of his extravagant lifestyle and because he continued to make life difficult for Scottish Protestants. In 1546, Beaton had executed a popular Protestant preacher, George Wishart. A few weeks later, in revenge for this action, a group of Protestants broke into St Andrews Castle and murdered Cardinal Beaton. Mary of Guise called on her own countrymen for help against the Scottish rebels and the murderers were besieged inside the castle until 1547, when they were starved into surrendering by French troops.

On the death of Henry VIII in 1547, the Earl of Hertford became the regent or 'Protector' of the young English king, Edward VI. The Protector then invaded Scotland, to renew English demands for a royal marriage between the English king and the Scottish queen, and defeated the Scots at the Battle of Pinkie. English troops were stationed up the east coast of Scotland, and their headquarters were at Haddington, near Edinburgh. In June 1548, a force of French troops landed at Leith, and besieged the English troops at Haddington. At the same time, the French fleet that had brought the soldiers, sailed back to France with Mary Queen of Scots on board. The Scots had agreed that Mary should marry the heir to the French throne, Francis, and that the queen mother, Mary of Guise, would rule as regent.

Questions

1. What were the consequences for Scotland of the Treaty of Greenwich?

2. Explain why Cardinal Beaton was murdered.

3. Read Source D on page 15 carefully and then answer the following questions.

   a. Why do the terms of this agreement look odd to a modern reader?
   b. Do you think that some Scots would not be happy with this agreement? Give a reason for your answer.
   c. Find out and write down how this agreement was broken.

The Reformation in Scotland grows

In 1525 the Scottish Parliament had passed a law banning Protestant books from being imported from other countries in Europe. However, Protestant ideas continued to spread throughout Scotland. Scottish merchants and sailors, who visited Europe on a regular basis, returned to their Scottish burghs with news of the religious developments that were taking place all over Europe. In the burghs, Protestants who criticised the wealth of the Catholic Church found an eager audience among the poor inhabitants of the burghs.

Those lairds, or landowners, who were unhappy at the taxes, or tithes, that they had to pay to the Catholic Church, began to listen to the arguments of the Protestant reformers. These lairds were unable to share in the wealth of the church in the way that the more powerful nobles could. For example, lairds were not close enough to the Stewarts and the royal court to have their children appointed to important positions in the Catholic Church.

⸻ *The execution of George Wishart*

Support for Protestant ideas also came from the Scottish earls, who felt that they had been excluded from Scottish government by the queen regent, Mary of Guise. The hostility of these nobles grew because they believed that too many French friends of the regent had been appointed to important positions in the government. To be a Scottish Protestant was thus to be a religious reformer, anti-French, anti-Catholic and opposed to the regent.

In particular, it was the execution of the Protestant preacher George Wishart in 1546 (see page 15) that led to the number of Protestants in Scotland growing more quickly. By the 1550s, there were Protestant congregations meeting in Scottish burghs, organised by former Catholic priests who had become Protestant preachers, or ministers. These Protestant clergymen used prayer books printed in English in their services; they read the Bible translated into English to their congregations; and they refused to say the Catholic mass in Latin, or any other language.

The mass

The mass represented everything that the Protestant reformers disliked about the Catholic Church. The mass was said in Latin, a language that few Christians understood; the congregation played little or no active part in the ceremony; and Catholics claimed that the priest turned the bread and wine into the body and blood of Jesus Christ, something that Protestants disputed.

17

(see page 15)

Source E

◄ *Lyne church, near Peebles, showing the plain, post-Reformation style.*

3 Mary Queen of Scots

The Lords of the Faithful Congregation

In 1558, unsigned 'Beggars' Summons' were nailed to the doors of religious communities in burghs across Scotland. These notices claimed that the Catholic friars who lived in these places were too rich, and that they were neglecting their duty to look after the poor (see Source A).

In 1559, Dundee and Perth announced that they were Protestant burghs. In the same year, Mary of Guise sent for more French troops to help her to deal with the growing number of Protestants who were demanding religious reform. A group of nobles and landowners, calling themselves the 'Faithful Congregation of Christ Jesus in Scotland', decided to oppose the regent's persecution of Scotland's Protestants.

The Lords of the Faithful Congregation, as this group were known, wanted the church in Scotland to become a Protestant church. They asked Elizabeth I, the new Queen of England and a Protestant, to help them defeat the French soldiers based in Scotland. First, Elizabeth sent money to help the Scottish Protestants and then, in 1560, the English navy sailed north to cut off supply routes to the French soldiers. The Lords of the Faithful Congregation said that they were loyal to Mary Queen of Scots, but that they were protecting their country from the French and defending Scottish Protestants from persecution.

When Mary of Guise died in July 1560, the crisis came to an end with the Treaty of Edinburgh. The terms of the treaty were:

Mary Queen of Scots's claim to the throne of England

Through her grandmother, Margaret Tudor, Mary Stewart had a good claim to the throne of England (see the family tree on page 5). Because many Catholics refused to recognise Henry VIII's divorce from his first wife, Catherine of Aragon, they saw his marriage to Anne Boleyn as illegal. This made Queen Elizabeth I of England, the daughter of Henty VIII and Anne Boleyn, illegitimate in their eyes. As far as those Catholics were concerned, Elizabeth had no claim to the English throne, but Mary Queen of Scots did.

- France and England agreed to withdraw their soldiers.
- Mary Queen of Scots would no longer claim to be Queen of England.
- The Scots would be left to sort out their own problems.
- The Scottish Parliament would meet to settle matters.

Scotland's Reformation Parliament met in Edinburgh in August 1560. The parliament agreed that the church, or kirk, in Scotland would be Protestant, and that the Pope would have no authority over the Church of Scotland. Also, the Catholic mass was forbidden in Scotland.

—— *Mary Queen of Scots returns from France, 1561*

In 1561, Mary Queen of Scots decided to return to Scotland after the death of her husband, King Francis II of France. As the Catholic queen of a Protestant country, Mary faced few religious crises because the Protestants were firmly in control of the Scottish church and there was little Catholic opposition. Rather, Mary's problems stemmed from political developments during her brief, personal reign that ended in 1567.

Questions

1. How do we know that Scotland was becoming a Protestant nation by 1560?

2. Why did the Lords of the Faithful Congregation ask England for help?

3. Why would Mary Queen of Scots have expected to face some problems when she returned to Scotland in 1561?

4. Read Source A carefully. Why do you think that it is unlikely that Scotland's beggars wrote the summons that appeared in 1558?

—— *Mary as Queen*

As a Catholic, Mary was allowed to attend mass in the privacy of her private, royal apartments. Some of her nobles plotted against her, but this was not unusual for a Scottish monarch. Instead, it was Mary's choice of a new husband that led to more serious difficulties. In 1565, Mary Queen of Scots married Henry Stewart, Lord Darnley.

—— *Lord Darnley – husband no 2*

Darnley was a distant cousin of Mary Queen of Scots and was second in line to the English throne after Mary (see family tree on page 5). Soon, Mary had given birth to an heir, called James, on 19 June 1566. In theory, her marriage should have been a successful alliance for the young queen, but within two years:

- her husband had been murdered
- Mary had remarried in a Protestant ceremony
- the Scottish nobles had rebelled and taken Mary prisoner
- Mary was forced to abdicate and her infant son became the new King of Scots.

Source B

▲ *Portrait of Mary Queen of Scots.*

19

This series of events was more disastrous for Mary personally than for her country, where the attractive, unpredictable young woman was probably seen as more trouble than a child monarch (the Scottish nobles were used to regents and to wielding their own power).

——— Murder, mystery and husband no 3

Mary Queen of Scots's downfall began with the murder of her second husband. Darnley had been ill, and it was thought that the fresh air at Kirk O' Field, on the outskirts of Edinburgh, would help him to regain his health. But early in the morning of 10 February 1567 there was an explosion at Darnley's house. His naked body was found in the garden and evidence suggested that he had been suffocated after the explosion had occurred.

Source C

The king's body was blown into the garden by the violence of the explosion. A poor English servant who slept in his room was killed there. The news spread quickly through the town. When the queen was told what had happened, she was greatly upset and stayed in her room all that day.

When Mary was a prisoner in England, her secretary wrote this description of how Mary reacted to the news of Darnley's murder.

Darnley's father charged and prosecuted James Hepburn, the Earl of Bothwell, for his son's murder. But Bothwell's supporters prevented a proper trial from taking place, and a month later Bothwell married Mary in a Protestant ceremony! Nobles were angry at Bothwell's dramatic attempt to seize power and gathered together an army to fight him and his supporters. While Bothwell escaped, Mary surrendered to her new husband's enemies and was sent to Lochleven Castle as a prisoner. There, it was discovered that Mary was pregnant, but she then had a miscarriage. The queen could have been pregnant before Darnley was murdered, and it was assumed that the father of the twin boys was Bothwell.

Mary had many enemies among her nobles, and these nobles now demanded that her infant son, James, be made king. Scotland would then be ruled by regents chosen from the nobility, until James was old enough to rule by himself. In July 1567, Mary's captors forced her to give up her throne (abdicate), and her son was crowned King James VI of Scotland. The following year, Mary escaped from Lochleven Castle, but her supporters were defeated at Langside and she fled to England. Queen Elizabeth I imprisoned Mary for the rest of her life. In 1586, after a Catholic plot against Elizabeth by people who wanted Mary as their monarch, Elizabeth ordered Mary's execution. Mary was executed at Fotheringay Castle in February 1587.

Bothwell escaped to Norway. He was arrested and handed over to the King of Denmark. He remained in prison in Norway until he died, in 1578.

Source D

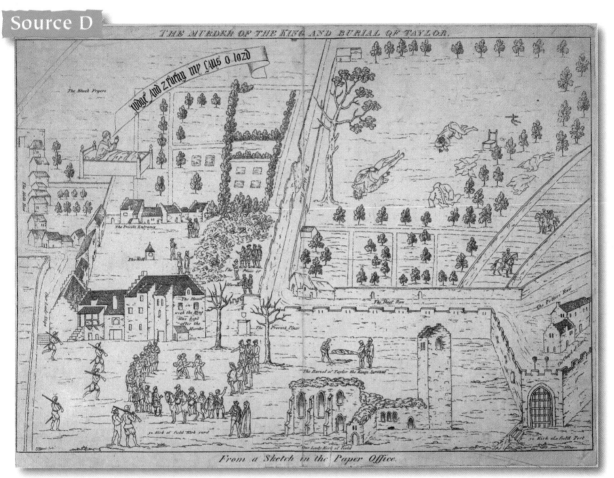

THE MURDER OF THE KING AND BURIAL OF TAYLOR.

From a Sketch in the Paper Office.

A drawing of the murder scene at Kirk O' Field in 1567.

Questions

1. Why do you think that many Scots had little or no respect for Mary after the scandal of Darnley's death?

2. Mary Queen of Scots spent most of her life either in France or in England. Why do you think that Mary is such a well-known person in Scottish history?

3. Read Source C carefully.

    a. Why is this a good source about the murder of Lord Darnley?
    b. Why might this source *not* be a useful source about the murder of Lord Darnley?
    c. Write down at least one reason why the information in the source may not be very accurate?

Extension task

1. In groups, discuss what you think seems to have been Mary's biggest mistake? Give at least two reasons for your answers.

Voyages of exploration

In 1450 Europeans knew little or nothing about two-thirds of the inhabited world. By the end of the sixteenth century, European explorers had visited the coasts of most of Africa and much of Asia, as well as North and South America. European merchants traded with the peoples of these newly-discovered markets and brought back spices, ivory, dyes for textiles, silk, porcelain, precious stones, and other new and exciting goods in exchange for European produce.

What made the explorers leave for unknown lands?

Many explorers set off on long, hard, dangerous sea voyages into the unknown. They were risking their lives, but they were attracted by:

- the chance to conquer new lands
- the opportunity to make a fortune from trade
- Catholic and Protestant missionaries were also keen to convert native peoples to their version of Christianity.

Developments in technology had made sea voyages more practical. The use of large, lateen or triangle-shaped sails made crossing the oceans less likely to end in disaster, as they could now deal with winds from most directions. More reliable compasses helped navigators to chart their progress and find their way across the world's vast oceans.

Once they arrived at new lands, European guns and cannon made it possible for explorers and merchants to enter the ports of the great African and Asian kingdoms and empires without being overpowered and captured. The peoples of North and South America did not have weapons and other technology that could prevent their kingdoms and empires from being conquered by ruthless Europeans.

Some European countries built small forts on these foreign shores, or 'trading factories', to buy and sell goods to the local inhabitants. Some Europeans decided to settle in the New World, as they called the Americas, and establish colonies from where they could look for gold, hunt animals for their fur (in Canada), and grow crops such as tobacco, cotton and sugar cane (in southern colonies in North America and islands in the Caribbean).

Why did the Scots stay closer to home?

The Scots played little or no part in the early phase of European exploration and colonisation. Their traditional trading areas were, to them, sufficient. During the sixteenth century Scottish merchants sold woollen cloth, animal skins, coal, lead ore and salt to markets in England, France, the Low Countries (Belgium and the Netherlands), Scandinavia (Norway, Sweden and Denmark) and the great trading ports of the Baltic Sea.

Apart from England, Scotland had not been at war with any other European country since 1266, so its trade had not been interrupted by costly conflicts. After the Reformation, Protestant Scotland remained on good terms with the Protestant states in Scandinavia and northern Europe, and Scottish trade with France tended to be with those areas where the French Protestant reformers, or Huguenots, were strong.

Journeys made by the great explorers.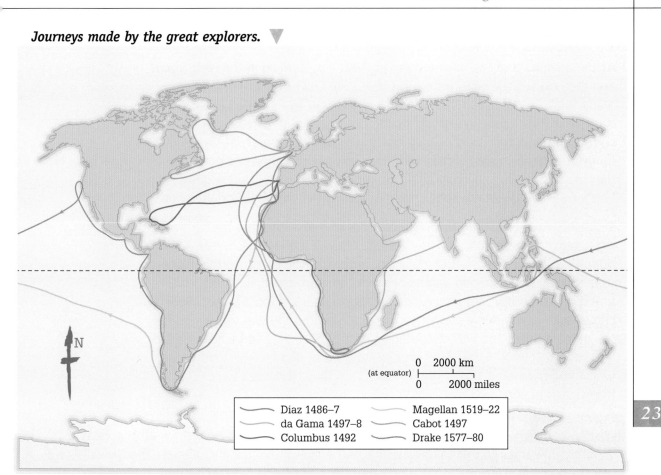

Diaz 1486–7

da Gama 1497–8

Columbus 1492

Magellan 1519–22

Cabot 1497

Drake 1577–80

23

Scottish merchants were also able to maintain good relations with England's enemies. During the relatively peaceful reign of James VI, Scottish trade enjoyed a period of prosperity that enabled the merchants to improve the harbours at Ayr, Dunbar, Elie, Dundee, Stonehaven and Peterhead.

In the 1620s, when many European states were expanding their territories, the Scots made an attempt to establish a colony in what they called 'Nova Scotia', the former French colony of Port Royal, in modern-day Canada. However, few Scots settled in the area and Charles I, who succeeded his father James VI, handed the territory back to the French in 1632. Scottish merchants thus failed to take advantage of the trading opportunities provided by the voyages of discovery of the fifteenth and sixteenth centuries. Scottish merchants, or more accurately, British merchants based in Scotland, would not make a mark on international trade until the late-seventeenth and early-eighteenth centuries.

Questions

1. What encouraged European explorers to sail to Africa, Asia and the Americas?

2. How did new and improved technology help explorers to sail around the world?

3. Why were Europeans in a few small ships able to escape capture by pirates or foreign ships as they sailed to Africa or Asia?

4. Why do you think very few Scots settled in Nova Scotia in the 1620s?

─── *What were Scottish burghs like?*

At the beginning of the sixteenth century most Scots lived in the countryside, and they made their living from farming. In the Lowlands, there were also many small towns, or burghs, which were busy centres for markets and traders. Scottish burghs were run by the burgesses, the merchants who controlled the burgh council. They made sure that the traders at the regular burgh markets and annual fairs paid their taxes or tolls, and did not cheat their customers. Each burgh had a tron, or weighing place, where goods bought at the market could be checked against the official burgh weights.

Sergeants were employed by burgh councils to make sure that the inhabitants of the burgh, and any visitors, obeyed the law. Each year, a small number of burgesses acted as bailies, or judges, in the burgh courts. Bailies usually fined or demanded apologies from criminals, but they could beat, brand or banish from the burgh anyone found guilty of most crimes. Serious crimes such as murder, were left to the local sheriff, who was appointed by the monarch. Begging was discouraged, and beggars had to be licensed by each burgh council. Many burghs were still surrounded by walls and gates which had been built in the Middle Ages, and these defences were maintained by the burgh councils.

24

Source A

Edinburgh and its port of Leith were the centre of Scottish trade to Europe. The capital, grown by the seventeenth century to be probably the second city in Great Britain, crammed its 40,000 inhabitants into half a square mile between the castle rock and Holyrood Palace. They lived in a manner more European than English, in tall tenements or 'lands', seven or more storeys high … The citizens, uttering the cry of 'gardy-loo' (gardez l'eau – watch out for the water), flung their sewage into the streets in a way that Englishmen found disgusting.

A modern historian describing Edinburgh at the end of the seventeenth century.

In each burgh, there were craftsmen who wove cloth, made shoes, tanned leather, and manufactured other goods for sale at the burgh markets. From about 1450 onwards, many craftsmen had organised themselves into craft guilds. There were guilds for most traditional crafts, such as fleshers (butchers), baxters (bakers), saddlers and cordiners (shoemakers). At a time when Scottish craftsmen were well known for the poor quality of their work the guilds were set up to try to improve the quality of Scottish trade, and to protect the interests of Scottish craftsmen against foreign imports.

Scottish tradesmen

Scottish tradesmen relied on making and selling goods cheaply to their local market. This typically consisted of poor Scots who could only afford the most basic goods, made with the cheapest materials. The wealthy lairds and nobles preferred foreign-made goods, and so did not help to improve local standards. To prevent the Scottish market being flooded with cheap foreign goods as well as expensive ones, Scottish tradesmen encouraged taxes and duties on foreign goods.

In smaller burghs, those farmers who lived in, or on, the outskirts of a burgh, were known as 'peasant burgesses'. However, most of the population of Scotland's burghs was made up of unfreemen (and women) and their families. These people were poor, and had few of the rights and privileges enjoyed by the burgesses. Many worked for the craftsmen and the wealthier merchants as labourers and servants. On the coast, they could find work as fishermen and sailors. In larger burghs, they sometimes earned a living as water carriers, prostitutes, or by selling ale.

Foreign influences?

By the end of the sixteenth century, foreign experts from England and the Low Countries (modern day Belgium and the Netherlands) were working in the textile industry in the east of Scotland. Some of these experts had come for the work opportunities in Scotland; others had been invited by churchmen. In 1611 some Dutch experts came to teach the Scots new techniques for manufacturing linen. There were also glass blowers from Venice working beside Scottish glass manufacturers. However, despite the example and new ideas of foreign craftsmen, the Scots were not inclined to abandon their traditional crafts for new skills and, by 1700, only the major Scottish industry of coal mining and the manufacture of linen cloth were flourishing. Apart from soap, refined sugar, glass, paper, rope, pottery and gunpowder, other manufactured goods were imported to Scotland from England and the rest of Europe.

Source B

► *Culross, and other well preserved burghs on the east of Scotland, remind us of Scotland's close links with northern Europe. The painted ceilings made from Scandinavian timbers in the grander houses, or 'palaces', and the church bells cast in the Netherlands or Sweden, are evidence of Scotland's North Sea trade links.*

25

Questions

1. How did burgesses encourage Scots to buy their goods at burgh markets?

2. In what ways did the burgh councils control everyday life in burghs?

3. Why was life for most people who lived in burghs very hard?

4. How did Scottish craftsmen try to improve the quality of their work by the end of the sixteenth century?

Extension task

1. Read Source A and then in groups discuss the following:

   a. What evidence is there that Edinburgh was an important place at that time?
   b. Why do you think that Edinburgh was more European than English at that time?

— Emigration and the 'plantations'

In the sixteenth century, there were many people in Scotland who wanted to emigrate (leave the country). Civil war, religious conflict and decades of rule by regents who failed to provide peace and security, seem to have prevented the Scots from taking advantage of the trading opportunities available at the end of the sixteenth century (see pages 22–3). The gap between rich and poor in Scotland was growing, and bad weather and poor harvests made life more difficult for farmers. Also, higher taxes and rising prices were reducing living standards for those craftsmen and unfreemen who lived and worked in Scotland's burghs. Whilst merchants who traded with Europe were comfortable, craftsmen and unfreemen were suffering.

During the reigns of Mary Queen of Scots and her son, James VI, there had been large-scale migration of Lowland Scots to Orkney and Shetland. These islands had the reputation of being new lands of opportunity because they were out of the reach of the royal government. In the 1560s, large numbers of Scots also travelled abroad to serve in foreign armies as mercenaries (see Source C on page 27). Scots fought in the French, Danish, Dutch and Swedish armies, as generals as well as ordinary soldiers. Some returned, but many never set foot in Scotland again.

26

Source C

Illustration of Scottish mercenaries during the Thirty Years' War.

'Plantations' in Ireland

By the end of the sixteenth century, wealthy merchants were able to enjoy a period of peace and prosperity that had not been seen for more than a century. This made them reluctant to take any risks that would endanger their wealth. However, Scots with ambition looked for adventure abroad. Some poorer lairds and less successful burgesses took advantage of the defeat of the O'Neills in County Down, and then the exile of the Earls of Tyrone and Tyrconnel in 1607 to move into Ulster. In 1609, 59 Scottish lairds and burgesses were granted 81,000 acres of land in the northeast of Ireland. Forty to fifty thousand Scots had been 'planted', or encouraged to settle in Ireland, by the middle of the seventeenth century. At that time, most of the Irish population was Catholic; most, but not all, of the Scottish settlers were Protestants.

At the same time as these 'plantations' in Ireland, thousands of Scots also emigrated to England, the Low Countries, Scandinavia, and sea ports around the Baltic. Most emigrants lost all contact with their homeland. Some Scottish traders became poor 'skottars', or stall-holders, who sold cheap goods at local markets throughout Scandinavia. Others became very wealthy merchants, marrying into the nobility of their new countries. Many descendants of the Scots who settled in Ireland later emigrated to English colonies in North America.

Questions

1. Give three reasons why so many Scots wanted to emigrate at the beginning of the seventeenth century.

2. Why do you think that many of the Scots who fought abroad as mercenaries never returned to Scotland?

3. Why did so many Scots settle in Ireland?

Union of crowns: James VI and I

—— *Regent after regent ...*

Although he was baptised in a Catholic ceremony as a baby in 1567, James VI was brought up as a Protestant. His foster parents, the Earl and Countess of Mar, ensured this. Crowned in July of that same year, when he was just one year old, James's personal rule of his kingdom did not begin until 1585, when he was 18. After his mother had abdicated in July 1567 (see page 20), Scotland was therefore governed by a series of regents (Moray, Lennox, Mar and Morton). Then, after 1578, various nobles controlled the young king until he was able to rule by himself, from 1585.

Scotland was torn apart during those years when King James was too young to rule by himself, by the feuding between the powerful families, all intent upon gaining power for themselves and imposing their own religious and political beliefs on the Scottish people.

At the end of 1567, the Scottish Parliament agreed that the Earl of Moray should be the regent of Scotland. However, in 1570, Moray was murdered by a supporter of the king's Catholic mother, Mary Queen of Scots. Those nobles who opposed the return of Mary to Scotland asked Elizabeth I of England to choose a new regent. She chose the Earl of Lennox, the father of Darnley. As regent, Lennox captured Dumbarton Castle and hanged the Catholic Archbishop Hamilton, who had remained loyal to Mary. In retaliation, in 1571, supporters of Mary attacked the parliament in Stirling and Lennox was killed. Next, the Earl of Mar became regent. He died a few months later so, in 1572, James Douglas, the fourth Earl of Morton, became the new regent.

Regent Morton managed to govern Scotland without being overthrown until 1578. In that year, James announced that he was old enough to rule his own kingdom. Morton then became the First Lord of the Council. However, Morton's enemies used a close friend of the young king and the French nephew of the Earl of Lennox, Esmé Stewart, to convince James that Morton had played a part in the murder of the king's father, Darnley. As a result, Morton was arrested in 1580 and executed the following year.

Source A

The young King James VI.

James VI – the 'wisest fool'?

James VI was well educated for the time. Under the guidance of his tutor, George Buchanan, he was taught subjects such as arithmetic, Greek, Latin, French, history, geography and astronomy. James VI liked to show off, and one noble is rumoured to have said that he thought the king was a fool. Another noble said that James must therefore be the 'wisest fool in Christendom' (that is, in all of western Europe), implying that he was actually a very shrewd man. However, like most educated men at that time, James VI was fascinated by witchcraft.

Witch hunts!

Many people in Europe during the sixteenth and seventeenth centuries were fascinated by tales of witchcraft. Even educated people believed in spells, curses and different forms of magic. In 1597, James VI wrote and published the *Daemonologie,* in which he put forward evidence that witches existed and that they were a danger to his kingdom.

This belief led James VI and his Scottish subjects to execute many so-called witches. At least 1000 witches were tortured and killed before the last execution of a Scottish witch in 1728. (This woman was accused of turning her daughter into a pony!) In England, with a population five times greater than that of Scotland, less than 1000 supposed witches were executed during the same period.

29

Source B

◀ *Illustration of a witch trial in Scotland, when those accused of witchcraft were said to have made a pact with the devil (seen on the left).*

Most victims of the witch-hunt were female. They tended to be old, widowed and poor. Sometimes a woman was accused of being a witch because of some physical feature that made her stand out: a large, prominent wart or mole on the face; walking with a limp; red hair (which was associated with Highlanders and the Irish). On most occasions, these women were accused of ridiculous crimes by their neighbours, such as killing a child by sticking pins in a wax doll, or making someone ill by firing invisible arrows at them.

Accusations of witchcraft tended to be made out of spite, in self-defence (to excuse some bad behaviour by the accuser), and to explain personal disaster or bad luck. Many Protestants in the sixteenth and seventeenth centuries did not want their personal problems to be seen as the result of God's will, or God's punishment: it was better to blame a witch for your misfortune. Once accused, the 'witches' were tortured to extract a confession. Then they were put to death by being tied to a stake or post, strangled, and then burned.

Case Study – witch trials

Dr John Fian was the schoolmaster at Saltpans in Lothian. He was arrested in 1590 and accused of being a member of a coven of witches in North Berwick. Witches were believed to operate in covens of thirteen, including one warlock, or male witch. Fian was tortured so that he would identify the other witches in his coven.

An account of Fian's torture was produced by Robert Pitcairn, writing in 1624.

To begin with, Fian had his head twisted or 'thrawn' with a rope. Then needles were driven under each of his fingernails. When he refused to confess, Fian was 'put to the most severe and cruel pain ... wherein he did abide so many blows that his legs were crushed and beaten together as small as might be ... whereby they were made unserviceable for ever'.

It was assumed that Dr Fian had not confessed because 'the devil had entered so deeply into his heart'. He was then taken to Edinburgh and, in January 1591, his body was tied to a stake, strangled and burned.

In 1596, a woman called Alison Balfour was accused of being a witch in a Scottish burgh. She was put in the 'cashielaws' (an arm-crushing vice) for two days, to make her confess. When she refused to confess to being a witch, her family were tortured with the 'pinniewinkis', or thumbscrews. Finally Alison confessed, so she was strangled and burned.

Questions

1. Who governed Scotland until James VI was old enough to rule his own kingdom?

2. What evidence is there to show that some Scots remained loyal to Mary as their queen?

3. Why do you think that James VI wanted to take revenge on his father's murderers?

4. Why did James VI think that finding and killing witches was necessary?

5. Why did people accuse their neighbours of being witches?

James VI of Scotland becomes James I of England

In 1589 James VI married Anne, the daughter of Frederick II of Denmark. The fifteen-year-old bride was eight years younger than James. Between 1594 and 1606 the royal couple had seven children. When the couple's eldest son, Henry, died, their second son, Charles, became heir to the throne. He would become Charles I when his father died in 1625.

▼ *Family tree of the Stuarts from the beginning of the seventeenth century.*

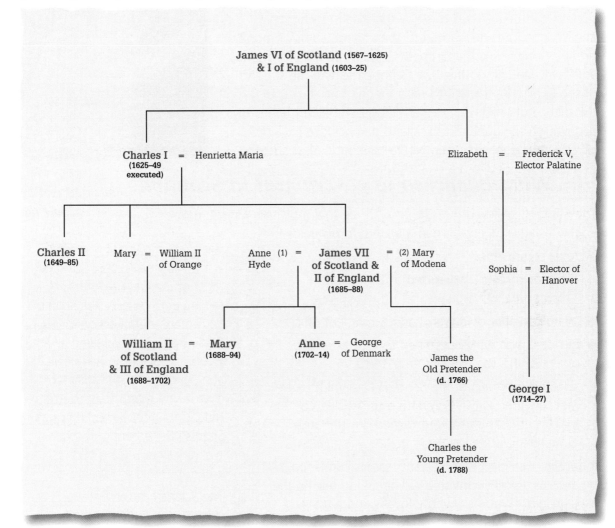

James VI of Scotland (1567–1625)
& I of England (1603–25)

Charles I = Henrietta Maria
(1625–49
executed)

Elizabeth = Frederick V,
Elector Palatine

Charles II (1649–85)

Mary = William II
of Orange

Anne (1) = James VII = (2) Mary
Hyde   of Scotland &   of Modena
                     II of England
                     (1685–88)

Sophia = Elector of
Hanover

William II
of Scotland
& III of England
(1688–1702)

= Mary
(1688–94)

Anne = George
(1702–14) of Denmark

James the
Old Pretender
(d. 1766)

George I
(1714–27)

Charles the
Young Pretender
(d. 1788)

31

In 1603, Queen Elizabeth I of England died, leaving no heir. James had a very strong claim to the English throne. His parents had been two of Elizabeth's closest relatives and before their own deaths, they had been first and second in line to the English throne. Above all, James VI was a Protestant, as Elizabeth I had been, so he had the support of important English politicians such as Lord Cecil. Three days after Elizabeth died, Cecil's messenger, Sir Robert Carey, arrived from London and knelt before James VI, King of Scots, to inform him that he was also James I, King of England and Ireland.

King James moves to England

When he became King James I of England and Ireland, James moved his family to England. After 1603 the Stewart monarchs seldom visited their Scottish homeland, although the kingdom continued to cause problems for them. James VI returned to Scotland on only one occasion, in 1617. Both Charles I and Charles II only went to Scotland to be crowned as King of Scots, at Edinburgh and Scone, respectively.

James I was determined to enjoy the wealth of his new English kingdom. He wanted to spend large sums of money on fine clothes, lavish apartments, and huge gifts for friends and favourites. To do this, James hoped to win the support of the English Parliament to raise money from taxes. His experience of ruling his northern kingdom helped James to deal with his opponents in England and achieve his aims. However, his son, Charles I, would have much less success.

Source C

▲ *King James VI and I in middle age.*

What happened to government in Scotland?

The Stewarts believed that they could rule their northern kingdom from England. James VI established a system to do this:

- royal commands
- the support of a small group of loyal nobles, called privy councillors
- a large number of lawyers and government officials
- bishops, who were appointed to look after the affairs of the Scottish kirk after 1610
- selected members of the Scottish Parliament, who met together as the Committee of Articles, to make sure that parliament carried out the absent monarch's wishes.

In running Scotland from England, James combined his skills as a politician with a willingness to rely on the assistance of favourites, whose loyalty and hard work were rewarded with promotion to the ranks of the nobility. Indeed, his reliance on favourites appeared to cause him more problems in England than in Scotland. As ruler of both kingdoms, James also quickly brought peace and stability to the Scottish border country. Between 1605 and 1621, James used a combined English-Scottish force to capture lawbreakers and end the cattle raids that had gone on for centuries between the English and Scots in that region.

The Scottish Parliament

In the sixteenth century and for most of the first half of the seventeenth century, the Scottish Parliament met in either Stirling or Edinburgh. Once Parliament House in Edinburgh had been completed in 1639, Parliament always met there. Scottish rulers tended to order a meeting of the Scottish Parliament only when it was strictly necessary, such as when they had to raise taxes.

The Scottish Parliament was supposed to represent the three estates of the kingdom: the clergy, the nobles and the burgesses, which met as a single group in a single chamber or room. From 1587, James VI extended representation to the shires or rural areas, to reduce the influence of the clergy from the Scottish kirk.

However, rather than learning to manage his English House of Lords and House of Commons, James increasingly chose to avoid dealing with Parliament. English resentment developed at James's skillful management of royal finances, which meant that he did not have to call on his English Parliament too often. This created problems for his son Charles when he became king. Charles I found it very difficult to win the support of his English Parliament whenever he needed its agreement, usually to grant him the tax revenues that he needed to finance his government.

After James VI had died, the wars and rebellions of the seventeenth century proved that the confidence of the Stewarts in ruling their northern kingdom by remote control had been misplaced. The Scots continued to pose problems for the dynasty's rulers.

Gunpowder plot, 1605

Guy Fawkes was born in York, in 1570. He became a Catholic and joined the Spanish army. In 1604 Fawkes returned to England and met up with some other Catholics in London, whose leader was Robert Catesby. Together with Fawkes, Thomas Wintour, Francis and Robert Tresham, and some others (see Source D on page 34), Catesby planned to blow up the Palace of Westminster on 5 November 1605. On that day, King James would be at Westminster to take part in the state opening of Parliament. Catesby hoped that the death of the king and the country's leading politicians would bring to an end the persecution of Catholics in England.

The conspirators put 36 barrels of gunpowder under the House of Lords. Because of his experience in the army and familiarity with explosives, Fawkes was given responsibility for setting off the explosives.

At the end of October 1605, a brother-in-law of the Treshams received an anonymous letter, telling him to stay away from Westminster on 5 November. This man passed the letter to the government, and Westminster was searched – the king's soldiers noticed an unusual amount of firewood in a cellar. At midnight on 5 November, a search party led by Sir Thomas Knevett discovered a man acting suspiciously. He claimed to be called 'John Johnson', but this man was in fact Guy Fawkes. When they searched him, they found that he was carrying fuses to set off an explosion.

33

Source D

Robert Winter · Christopher Wright · John Wright · Thomas Percy · Guido Fawkes · Robert Catesby · Thomas Winter · Bates

Guy Fawkes and the plotters.

34

Once Guy Fawkes had been captured, the other conspirators were soon rounded up. After being tortured on the rack, each of them confessed to their part in the plot. Their trial took place in Westminster Hall, and the king is supposed to have watched from a secret hiding place. The plotters were sentenced to be dragged through the streets of London, and then hanged, beheaded and quartered at Westminster, in January 1606. James I found that he was more popular than ever with his new subjects: having foiled a Catholic plot against king and parliament, his credentials as a Protestant monarch were guaranteed.

Questions

1. Why did James VI become the King of England and Ireland? Look at the family tree on page 5 to help you with your answer.

2. Would it be fair to say that James VI abandoned Scotland when he became James I of England and Ireland? Give a reason for your answer.

3. How did James VI rule Scotland from London?

4. Use the information above, and any other sources available, to tell the story of the Gunpowder Plot in your own words. A good approach would be:

   ● introduce the plotters, and their reasons for planning to blow up king and parliament

   ● tell the story of the plot, and why it failed

   ● describe what happened to the plotters, and the effect that the plot had on the popularity of James VI and I.

6

The Covenanters defy the king

A Presbyterian church

A long time in the making

The religious and political conflicts of the seventeenth century had long-lasting effects on the Scottish nation. For example, between 1652 and 1660, the Stewart dynasty was expelled from Scotland and the former kingdoms of Scotland and England were united into a single, united republican state (there was no monarch). Also, it was not until 1690 that the Presbyterian character of the Church of Scotland, or kirk, was finally established. This happened when the Protestant daughter of James VII, Mary, and her Protestant husband, William, became king and queen. Their acceptance of a Presbyterian Church of Scotland ended nearly a century of conflict between the English-based Stewart dynasty and their Scottish subjects, who objected to the Stewarts' religious policies. From James VI to his grandson, James VII, the Stewarts had insisted that the Church of Scotland should model itself on the Church of England.

Case Study – What does Presbyterian mean?

From the beginning of the reform movement in the sixteenth century, Protestant reformers wanted the church in Scotland to be Presbyterian in its practices and theology. This meant that they wanted there to be no bishops in the church in Scotland. The Catholic mass had already been abandoned, and the celebration of traditional holy days, such as Christmas and Easter, was discouraged. In most respects, the Scottish kirk was similar to other churches in the kingdoms of northern Europe, such as the reformed church in Denmark (although these churches did have bishops).

- At the heart of Scottish Presbyterian services was the minister's sermon, based on readings from the Bible.

- In some parishes, prayers were not written down or printed, but were composed by ministers for each service.

- A great deal of effort went towards keeping the Sabbath, or Sunday, holy.

- Communion services were held much less often than in Catholic churches, and they were much less formal affairs.

- In each parish, congregations were supposed to elect their ministers. There were no bishops, but the early Protestant Church had superintendents who carried out many of the duties and responsibilities of bishops, as local governors or administrators.

Kirk sessions (councils) in the parishes were very powerful. They were made up of the minister and a group of elders and deacons, who were elected as parish officials from the congregation each year. Church discipline was very strict: 'searchers' hunted out people who failed to attend church on the Sabbath, and 'noters' reported on people who swore or used bad language.

Kirk sessions could fine parishioners who had broken the rules and make them stand by the 'pillar of repentance' in sackcloth and ashes. For some offences, parishioners could be put in the jougs or branks (the first, an iron collar attached to a pillar; the second, an iron cage worn over the head – see Source A on page 36). Others were sent to the Correction House, to be beaten and fed on bread and water.

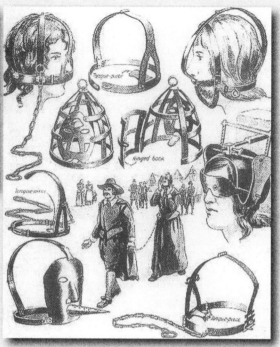

▲ *Jougs, which were iron neck rings, and branks* ▶ *, which was an iron cage that fitted around the head and over the tongue, were used as punishments by the ministers of the reformed church.*

— The Scottish kirk

During the reign of Mary Queen of Scots, who was a Catholic, the Scots had no Protestant monarch to act as head of the national church in Scotland. The early Protestant kirk therefore held a council, or General Assembly. This council was designed to represent much the same groups who met at the Scottish Parliament – the nobles and lords, the burgesses, the superintendents and some ministers.

Andrew Melville

After the Protestant reformer John Knox died in 1572, the dominant figure in the Scottish church was Andrew Melville. He had lived in Switzerland for six years, and had become a follower of the Calvinist Theodore Beza. In 1574, he became principal of the University of Glasgow. Melville was opposed to the Church of Scotland having bishops. He wanted the General Assembly to consist only of ministers and elders. Above all, he believed that the government had to do what the church wanted in the case of religious and moral matters.

Portrait of Andrew Melville. ▶

Bishops or no bishops?

Between 1578 and 1612, there were fierce arguments between James VI, the General Assembly and parliament over how the Scottish kirk should be organised. In 1578 the General Assembly voted narrowly to accept Melville's ideas (see box on page 36). However, the Scottish Parliament refused to accept these proposals, and in 1584 the government said that bishops would be retained in the Scottish kirk. Then, in 1592, parliament removed from the bishops all power over the administration and government of the kirk. But, in 1612, James VI ordered that the power of bishops should be restored in the Church of Scotland. By the Five Articles of Perth in 1618, James restored some religious practices that had been abandoned by Protestants in Scotland, such as kneeling to receive communion.

In the 1630s, when Charles I was on the throne, the nobles and lairds of Scotland became concerned that Charles would carry out his threat to take back all of the land that had belonged to the Church of Scotland before 1540. Charles had found himself short of money, but he did not want to be dependent upon his English Parliament to raise taxes on his behalf. Confiscating these church properties in Scotland would raise a great deal of money for the royal treasure chest. At the same time, merchants and manufacturers in Scottish burghs were unhappy at the growing burden of taxes that the king was imposing on them.

The nobles, lairds, manufacturers and merchants were also united in their opposition to the king's plans to make the Church of Scotland more like the Church of England. They knew that Charles I intended to impose the use of a prayer book on the Scottish church, similar to the prayer book used by his subjects in England, without consulting its General Assembly in Scotland.

The prayer book riot

In 1637, Charles I decided to introduce a new prayer book in the Scottish church, to replace the Book of Common Order that had been used by Scottish congregations since the reign of Mary Queen of Scots. The new prayer book contained references to the celebration of saints' days and festivals such as Christmas and Easter, and to the use of 'ornaments' (possibly statues) in kirks. To most Scots these sections were attempts to impose Catholic practices on the kirk. On 23 July 1637, an attempt to introduce the use of the prayer book at the great kirk of St Giles in Edinburgh started a riot (see Source C on page 38). This was followed by numerous protests throughout the country against the introduction of the prayer book. What annoyed the Scots most of all was the fact that Charles I had not discussed the matter with the General Assembly, or the Scottish Parliament.

37

Source C

The Arch-Prelate of St Andrewes in Scotland reading the new Service-booke in his pontificalibus assaulted by men & Women, with Cricketts stooles Stickes and Stones.

▲ *A contemporary illustration of the prayer book riot showing the Archbishop of St Andrews being attacked by his congregation.*

How did the Covenanters spark off the English Civil War?

In 1638, Scottish nobles, burgesses and ministers met at Greyfriars Kirk in Edinburgh where they signed an agreement, or contract, called the National Covenant. This document declared that those who signed the covenant were opposed to any change in their worship that was not approved by free assemblies or Parliament. They promised to defend Scotland's religion against anyone who tried to attack it.

Fearing that Charles I would send an army to Scotland to deal with those who opposed his religious policies, the Covenanters, as they became known, recruited an army. The army included many Scottish soldiers who had gained great experience fighting for the Swedish king in Europe. Seizing the initiative, in 1640 the Scots marched into the north of England and occupied Newcastle, before Charles could send an army north.

Charles I had to summon his English Parliament to raise the taxes needed to finance a campaign to defeat the Scottish rebels. The members of this Parliament belonged to what became known as the 'Long Parliament', because it lasted for such a long time whilst it struggled to limit the king's power.

Source D

◄ *Portrait of Charles I painted in 1631.*

At that time, Charles I also wanted to command an army to defeat a rebellion in Ireland, but he was thwarted by parliament. To achieve his aims, Charles then tried to arrest five members of parliament as they sat in the House of Commons! He failed to arrest them, so he moved his royal court to Oxford. From this base, Charles plotted to defeat his enemies in parliament by force. This military campaign against his parliamentary opponents marked the beginning of the English Civil War and, in the short term, it was the Scottish Covenanters who had sparked it off. In England, those who supported the king fought a bloody war against the Parliamentarians and their supporters.

The period of the Civil War was marked by dreadful cruelty towards rivals and opponents. In 1644, supporters of the king, commanded by the Marquis of Montrose, were allowed to loot and burn the city of Aberdeen, in revenge for the death of a drummer boy. When the Covenanter troops, led by General Leslie, defeated the army of Montrose at the Battle of Philipshaugh in 1645, the victors killed all their prisoners, including women and children.

The Solemn League and Covenant

In 1643 the leaders of the Scottish and English rebels who opposed the rule of King Charles I signed a Solemn League and Covenant. This agreement said that the Church of England and Ireland should be a Presbyterian Church, similar to the type of church the Covenanters wanted for Scotland. In return, the Scots accepted the terms of the Westminster Confession of 1643 that was drawn up at a conference in London. This document set out how Protestants in the United Kingdom should worship, what they should believe, and how their congregations should be organised. The General Assembly of the Church of Scotland accepted the terms of the Confession in 1645, and these terms became the foundation of the religious principles of the Kirk, lasting to the present day.

Questions

1. What made Charles so unpopular in Scotland?

2. How do we know that the king might find the Covenanters difficult to defeat?

3. Why did Charles I have to rely on his English Parliament to defeat the Covenanters?

Source exercise

Source E

It is our pleasure that all the lords Archbischops and Bischops within our Kyngdome off Scotland sall in all publick places weare gownes with standing capes and cassocks, and the inferiour clergue especiallie after they have taiken the degree off doctours or bachelours in divinitie or be preachours in any toune sall weare the same habite for faschioun bot for worth according to thair meanes, and no tippets unless they be doctors ...

In 1633, Charles I ordered ministers in the Scottish Kirk to wear the same clothes as those worn by clergymen in the Church of England. These were some of the instructions.

1. Do you think that it is useful to read the source with its original spelling? Give a reason for your answer.

2. List three words that look as if they describe items of clothing, e.g. 'gownes'.

3. Do you think that Charles I wanted to fall out with the members of the Scottish kirk? Again, give a reason for your answer.

40

Source A

A contemporary painting of the execution of Charles I in 1649.

England rejects the Stewart dynasty ...

In 1646 the Scots captured Charles I at Newark and handed him over to his English opponents at Newcastle. He was taken south, and later tried and executed in 1649. This event shocked most Scots, and soon the relationship between the rebels in Scotland and England broke down. In England, the monarchy and the House of Lords were abolished, and a republic was established (England no longer had a king or queen). All power was in the hands of Parliament, which would rule the Commonwealth – a term used to describe the country, now that it was no longer a kingdom with a king or queen. Within a short period of time, Oliver Cromwell (1599–1658), who had been one of the king's chief critics in the English Parliament and a commander of the Commonwealth's army, was declared Lord Protector of England. In many ways, Cromwell was as powerful as any Stewart monarch had ever been, as the Scots would soon discover to their cost.

... but the Scots crown Charles II

Charles, eldest son of the executed Charles I, landed in Scotland in the summer of 1650. He had fled abroad when his father had been captured by his enemies. In an effort to win the support of the Scots for his cause to regain his dynasty's throne, Charles accepted the terms of the Solemn League and Covenant. In January 1651, he was crowned Charles II, King of Scots, at Scone. This was a signal to the Commonwealth forces in England that the Stewarts were back. With the backing of a Scottish army, they could pose problems for the new government in England.

Experienced English forces, led by Oliver Cromwell, inflicted devastating defeats on the Scots at Dunbar in September 1650 (see Sources B and C), then at Worcester in September 1651. Charles II escaped capture and fled to safety on mainland Europe. Then, in October 1651, the Commonwealth government of England declared that Scotland and England were a single Commonwealth, or state! In January 1652, the burghs and shires of Scotland were ordered to elect representatives to meet and agree to the union of both countries.

Source B

◀ *The New Model Army defeating the Scottish army led by General Leslie at Dunbar.*

Source C

On 22 July 1650, Oliver Cromwell marched into Scotland at the head of a 16,000 strong army ... the Protector's troops were well drilled, well disciplined – and paid. His New Model Army was the first permanent military force to be seen in Britain. It was the beginning of a new era in soldiering. Hitherto, armies had been created from the 'host' – ordinary working men of fighting age who were obliged to fight for their country for up to 40 days in any one year.

Description by a modern historian of Cromwell's New Model Army when it invaded Scotland.

Source D

▶ *Portrait of Oliver Cromwell dating from 1649.*

General Monck and the army take control

In 1653 the Commonwealth abolished the General Assembly of the Church of Scotland, and forced the Scots to accept that religious tolerance should be permitted, so long as it did not extend to bishops and Catholics. The Commonwealth army that occupied and controlled Scotland had a strength of 36,000 in 1652, but this was reduced to 10,000 in subsequent years, as five large forts or citadels were built at Leith, Inverness, Inverlochy, Perth and Ayr. These fortresses were not built to defend Scotland from enemies, but to establish military control over the Scots.

From 1654 the occupying forces were under the control of General Monck. To support him further, Oliver Cromwell introduced a new network of Justices of the Peace, to maintain law and order. However, Monck maintained his authority through his New Model Army.

What was the Scots' reaction to Monck's leaving?

Cromwell died in 1658, and the government of his son, Richard, proved to be unpopular and short-lived. Powerful men in England decided to invite Charles Stewart to return from exile and restore the monarchy in England (Charles had lived abroad since his defeat at Worcester in 1651).

In 1660 Monck marched his large occupation force south from Scotland. He intended to use his troops to support the restoration of the monarchy in England. On his departure, a group of representatives of the Scottish burghs and shires pleaded with Monck to maintain the union of Scotland and England. This was because the order and stability of foreign, military occupation appeared to have found its supporters among some of Scotland's merchants and manufacturers. However, most of Scotland's traders hoped that the restoration of the Stewart monarchy would lead to a revival in Scotland's trade with traditional markets such as France and the Netherlands, who were England's rivals.

In May 1660, Charles Stewart returned to England from his foreign exile. He ruled his kingdoms as Charles II until his death in 1685.

43

Questions

1. Why were the Scots and English at war in 1650?

2. Read Source C. How does the historian suggest that not all soldiers in the seventeenth century were paid?

3. Why was the New Model Army different from all previous armies in Britain?

4. Why did the Commonwealth abolish the General Assembly of the Scottish Kirk?

—— *Charles turns against the Presbyterians*

Fearing that Charles II had forgotten his pledge to support the Solemn League and Covenant, a group of protesters met in Edinburgh in 1660 to discuss how best to remind the king that he had promised to give his support to a Presbyterian Church of Scotland. When their leader was arrested and executed by the king's officials in Edinburgh, it was clear that the demands of the Covenanters would not be achieved by the restoration of the Stewart dynasty. Charles had no intention of meeting the demands of Scotland's Presbyterians, and he would not keep the promises that he had made to the Scots in 1650 regarding their religious freedom.

Charles II also appointed bishops and took away the right of church congregations to elect their own ministers. Rather than obey the king, three hundred ministers abandoned their churches and held open-air services or conventicles. They risked torture and execution, as did congregations who supported them. Sentries were posted at conventicles to warn of the approach of the king's troops.

In 1679 Archbishop Sharp of St Andrews was murdered at Magus Moor. The murderers then joined with conventiclers from South Lanarkshire. This force of 40 men on horseback, and 200 on foot, defeated an army of professional troops, led by Graham of Claverhouse, at Drumclog near Strathaven. After occupying Glasgow, these Covenanters and their supporters were defeated at the Battle of Bothwell Brig by a royal army led by the Duke of Monmouth, an illegitimate son of the king. Royal power, in the form of superior armed forces, proved to be strong enough to defeat Scotland's religious rebels.

Source A

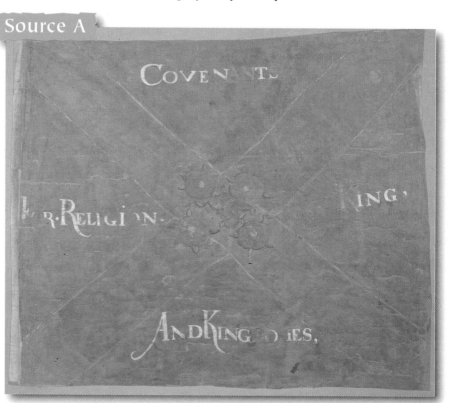

COVENANT
R·RELIGION·
KING·
AndKINGDOMES,

A banner carried by the Covenanters in 1679. ▶

The 'killing times'

The defeated Covenanters were imprisoned in Edinburgh, and most were allowed to return home, so long as they promised not to take up arms against the king again. As a punishment, a small group of Covenanters who refused to accept this agreement were sentenced to be transported to the West Indies as forced labour. However, most of the captives died before their prison ships crossed the Atlantic.

Later in 1679, the Duke of Monmouth was replaced by the king's brother, the Duke of York (soon to be James VII), and the persecution of Covenanters who opposed the king's religious policies began. This period is sometimes called the 'killing times', when Highland troops loyal to the monarchy hunted down conventiclers and their ministers. The Highland troops were less interested in religious debate, than the opportunity to seek employment as paid troops in the Lowlands. However, most historians suggest that the number of killings has been exaggerated and was probably in the tens, rather than hundreds.

What was left of the Covenanters was led by three men – one of Archbishop Sharp's murderers, Hackston of Rathillet; Donald Cargill; and Richard Cameron. They were defeated at Airds Moss in 1680: Cameron was killed and Hackston was captured, and later executed; Cargill was captured and executed in 1681. What was left of the Cameronians, as they called themselves, found a new leader in James Renwick. They continued to fight a hit-and-run guerrilla war against government forces for several years. In 1688, Renwick was captured and executed.

William and Mary accept a Presbyterian Church of Scotland

Many years of religious conflict in Scotland came to a sudden end in 1690, when King William and Queen Mary came to the throne. In that year, the Presbyterian Church of Scotland, with its General Assembly and no bishops, was accepted by the government. The process of reforming the church in Scotland, that had begun in the reign of Mary Queen of Scots, was finally completed.

Questions

1. How, in 1660, did Charles II show that he had forgotten the promises he had made to the Scots in 1650?

2. Why did many ministers abandon their churches to hold open-air services?

3. What happened to the Covenanters who were taken prisoner at Bothwell Brig?

4. Why do you think the period is known as the 'killing times'?

5. How did the Church of Scotland become Presbyterian in 1690, once and for all?

How did James VII upset the Scots?

When Charles II died in 1685, his brother, the Duke of York, became James VII, King of Scots, and James II of England (see family tree on page 31). James had become a Catholic, and this would lead to major difficulties during his short reign. As king, he had to promise to defend the rights of the Protestant churches in both Scotland and England, despite his own religious beliefs. Most of his subjects did not believe in religious toleration, and most believed that, as a Catholic, like his second wife, Mary of Modena, James would attempt to restore the Pope's authority over the Church of Scotland and the Church of England.

Source B

James VII and II.

A male heir

In 1688, Mary of Modena, the second wife of James VII, gave birth to a son. This son was heir to the throne, since a male child took precedence over his two older, Protestant half-sisters, Mary and Anne (born when their father had been married to Anne Hyde – see family tree on page 31). It was assumed that this boy would be brought up as a Catholic, and so it would be likely that Stewart monarchs would continue to be Catholic in the future.

46

The Scots call a Convention

In 1688, there was an uprising in England against James VII and II, and he fled his throne in what is called the Glorious Revolution. In Scotland, a parliament met in April 1689 to discuss the crisis, in part caused by the birth of a royal heir who would be brought up as a Catholic. This Parliament was called a Convention Estates because it had not been ordered to meet by the absent king, who had fled abroad. The Convention declared that James VII was not fit to rule over his Scottish subjects, since he was a Catholic. Also, according to the Claim of Right (a list of charges against the king, drawn up by the Convention), James was found guilty of many crimes against his subjects.

The Convention claimed that the Scottish Parliament could now pass laws without royal interference, and that the monarch had no right to change laws passed by parliament. The Committee of the Articles was abolished, as it gave the king or queen too much power over parliament's business. The Convention also declared that the Church of Scotland was a Presbyterian church. In fact, the throne of Scotland was to be offered to Mary, the elder of the two Protestant daughters of James VII, and her Protestant husband, William of Orange (see family tree on page 31). William and Mary accepted this offer, and agreed to respect the decisions passed by the Scottish Parliament.

‘Bonnie Dundee’

John Graham of Claverhouse, Viscount of Dundee, was a supporter of James VII. He was known to his friends and enemies as either ‘Bonnie Dundee’ or ‘Bluidy Clavers’ (‘Bloody Claverhouse’). He was hated by Lowlanders for the way that he had persecuted Covenanters in the ‘killing time’ (see page 45). In 1689, Graham gathered an army of Highlanders and defeated a Convention army at the narrow Pass of Killiecrankie. Dundee was able to call on the support of those clan chiefs and their clansmen who did not agree with the decision to invite William and Mary to replace James VII as the Scottish monarch. Dundee was killed during the battle, and his force was finally defeated at Cromdale on 1 May 1690. This brief but bloody civil war saw the defeat of the Jacobite forces in Scotland loyal to the exiled King James (or Jacobus, in Latin).

When the two daughters of James, Mary and Anne, died, the succession passed to distant cousins from the House of Hanover in Germany (see family tree on page 31). Subsequent attempts by the Jacobites to place James, the son of James VII, on the throne of what was now the United Kingdom, failed.

Source C

Portrait of ‘Bonnie Dundee’. ▶

47

Questions

1. Why did the religious beliefs of James VII cause him difficulties?

2. How did the birth of a son and heir increase the difficulties facing James VII?

3. Why were the Convention Estates so hostile to James VII? Give two reasons.

4. Why do you think that John Graham had two such different nicknames: ‘Bonnie Dundee’ and ‘Bluidy Clavers’?

5. Why was the death of John Graham, and the defeat of his army, an important turning point in the history of the Stewart dynasty?

The Convention had enlisted the aid of English forces to defeat the army of Bonnie Dundee in 1690 (see page 47). Religious conflict in the seventeenth century had reduced support for the Catholic members of the Stewart dynasty to inhabitants of remote glens and islands.

What was life like as part of a clan?

The clan system

The clan system had been changing and adapting since before James IV had attacked the power and influence of the Lord of the Isles (see page 4). As the lands of the Campbells and Gordons were enlarged, many Highlanders had become tenants who rented land from distant clan chiefs, or local tacksmen, who had been given the right to collect rents in that area. Highland farmers had little or no loyalty to these landlords. In the more isolated glens, and remote islands, closer links between chiefs and tenants were preserved.

Highland farming

Most Highlanders were poor, subsistence farmers who were the sub-tenants of the local landowner. The landowner might be the chief, or one of his tacksmen. The tacksmen or chiefs' tenants grew crops such as oats and barley, and kept goats, sheep and a few black cattle. Often, their rents were paid in the form of goods or produce, or even cattle. The sub-tenants paid their rents to the tacksmen by working on their land, free of charge.

Chiefs hoped to sell the clan's surplus cattle at Lowland markets, and professional drovers were skilled in driving herds of black cattle. However, these same drovers were sometimes used to steal cattle from other clans. The threat of cattle theft was enough to force some clans to pay blackmail money to their neighbouring clans for many years, to protect their cattle from theft.

Farmers in the Highlands faced many problems:
- the weather was often cold, and wet in summer, which made it difficult to grow crops
- there was a shortage of fertile soil in most glens
- too many cattle grazed on too little pasture
- traditional, subsistence farming methods could not feed a growing population.

Fertile land was divided into long strips known as rigs. These rigs were shared out between the tenants and sub-tenants, and rotated regularly, to make sure that everyone could work on the best land.

When battles were fought, the chief knew he could call on his tenants to fight as part of his army. Many chiefs measured their own importance by the number of fighting men (their own tenants) that they could command.

Highland life and culture

Apart from Argyll and Perthshire, few Presbyterian ministers preached in the Highlands and Islands. Many Highland glens were allowed by their Jacobite landlords to remain loyal to the bishops appointed before William III and Mary had replaced James VII. Other glens, and some islands, had been converted to Catholicism by missionaries. But many Highland areas were served by neither ministers nor priests. As a result, the Scottish Society for the Propagation of Christian Knowledge was founded by Lowland Scots, in 1709. Its purpose was to set up Highland schools where reading, writing, arithmetic and religious knowledge could be taught in English.

Half the population of Scotland is thought to have been Gaelic-speaking in 1500. Gaelic as an everyday language was not confined to the Highlands and Islands, as much of Galloway and Carrick were still Gaelic-speaking at that time. However, from the reign of James VI, the sons of clan chiefs began to be educated in the Lowlands. Gaelic traditions were gradually lost as books, songs, and even legal documents, were written and published in English. Also, the chiefs and their families took pride in their knowledge of the fashions and culture of the Lowlands, and of countries abroad. Although clan chiefs continued to encourage bards, or storytellers, to preserve clan songs and legends, and pipers still played for their chiefs at home and in battle, other features of clan life were fast disappearing. Few sub-tenants were able to enjoy the rich culture that had been developed by Highland clans over the previous 1500 years.

Source A

Highland piper.

49

Question

1. Using the information that you have read so far, and any other resources that are available, write a description of life in the Highlands at the end of the seventeenth century.

Consider:

- how the clans were organised
- the differences between the tenants and sub-tenants of the chiefs
- farming methods in the Highlands
- the importance of the cattle trade
- religion in the Highlands
- art and culture in the Highlands.

Campbell v MacDonald

In the sixteenth and seventeenth centuries, at least one-third of the Scottish population lived in the Highlands and Islands. At the end of the seventeenth century, many of the inhabitants continued to speak Gaelic, and the loyalties and traditions of tribal or clan society had not died out completely. Many Lowland Scots called the Highlanders 'Irish', and this suggests that the Lowlanders did not consider the inhabitants of northern and western Scotland to be 'Scottish', like themselves.

In 1691, many Scots accepted the fact that they were now ruled by Mary, the daughter of James VII, and her husband, William III. However, the new monarchs did not believe that they could rely on the loyalty of many of their Highland subjects. Many chiefs were Jacobites, and believed that James VII was their rightful king. The new king and queen's chief representative in Scotland was John Dalrymple, the Master of Stair. He instructed John Campbell, Earl of Breadalbane, to talk to the Jacobite clan chiefs and try to persuade them to switch their support to the new king and queen, in order to prevent them from rebelling again. In this, Campbell was unsuccessful.

Taking the oath of loyalty to William and Mary

As persuasion had failed, the Master of Stair, as Secretary of State for Scotland, ordered all Jacobite chiefs to take an oath of loyalty to King William III and Queen Mary. This oath had to be made before the end of December 1691 at Fort William. Those who failed to take the oath risked punishment at the hands of the army.

Maclain, Chief of the MacDonalds of Glencoe, was late in making his promise. He was not the only chief who did not take the oath before the deadline. Maclain had delayed his promise for several months, waiting for James VII, who was living in France, to give the Jacobite chiefs permission to swear an oath of loyalty to William and Mary. Only when this permission had been granted did Maclain go to Fort William to swear the oath. However, on arriving there he found that there was no one to take his oath. He was told to go to Inverary, and swear his oath in front of Campbell of Ardkinglass, the sheriff of Argyll. On his way to Inverary, Maclain was delayed for one day by an officer of Argyll's Regiment. When he reached Inverary on the 2 January, he discovered that the sheriff had gone to visit relatives for Hogmanay. When the sheriff returned, he allowed Maclain to take the oath on 6 January 1692, a week late.

Treachery!

Stair advised William to punish Maclain's clan for not taking the oath in time, and William agreed to an attack on the MacDonalds. British troops stationed at Fort William were selected to carry out the order. Robert Duncanson, a major in the Earl of Argyll's Regiment, sent Robert Campbell of Glenlyon and 120 of his troops to Glencoe. Most of these soldiers were members of Clan Campbell.

In 1689, the MacDonalds of Glencoe and Keppoch had joined 'Bonnie' Dundee's rebellion. When 'Bonnie' Dundee was killed, the MacDonalds had returned home to their glens. The MacDonalds' traditional rivals, the Campbells, had not joined the rebels who supported King James VII. As they had made their way home, the MacDonalds had helped themselves to the horses, sheep, cattle and goats of Robert Campbell of Glenlyon.

For two weeks the soldiers lived in Glencoe and enjoyed the hospitality of the Macdonalds and Maclain. Although the Campbells and the Macdonalds were sworn enemies, Highland custom said that all hostilities should stop if hospitality was offered and accepted. Then, on the morning of 13 February 1692, the soldiers were ordered to attack the clanspeople. 38 clan members were killed. Maclain was shot dead in his bedroom as he dressed to say goodbye to his guests – he thought that they were leaving! Duncanson and reinforcements from Fort William arrived two hours after the massacre. This delay allowed as many as 450 MacDonalds to escape. The reinforcements were not able to block the exits from the glen, and most of Maclain's people were able to get away.

Source B

▲ *The Glencoe massacre, as painted by a Victorian painter in the nineteenth century.*

Source C

You are hereby ordered to fall upon the rebels, the MacDonalds of Glencoe, and put all to the sword under seventy. You are to take special care that the old fox and his sons upon no account escape your hands.

Extract from the orders Duncanson sent to Robert Campbell of Glenlyon.

The massacre of men, women and children by British troops was an outrage. Also, the king had made a serious error of judgment. Stair eventually had to resign, but William III supported him until 1695, even making him an Earl! Many Highland clans had little or no respect for the new king and queen, and now, as a result of the massacre, support in the Highlands for the Jacobite cause received a great boost.

Extension task

Some Scots were horrified, and others were delighted, to hear the news of the Glencoe massacre. Use the information in this book, and any other resources that are available, either in your class, in the school or local library, or on the internet, to write a one-sided or biased description of what happened at Glencoe in 1692.

You can choose to be either a Jacobite, or a supporter of William and Mary.

A Jacobite would mention:

- Maclain's loyalty to James VII
- Maclain's attempts to swear the oath in time, his bad luck on his travels to Fort William and Inverary, the fact that he swore the oath to be loyal to the new monarchs
- Maclain's hospitality to the soldiers who visited the glen
- the horror of the massacre
- the new king's attitude towards the Master of Stair.

A supporter of William and Mary would mention:

- Maclain's deliberate failure to swear the oath in time
- the threat posed to law and order by Jacobite clans
- the fact that most of the clan escaped
- the new king's support for the Master of Stair.

10 *The Darien Disaster*

The Company of Scotland

As early as 1661, the English Navigation Acts stated that goods and produce being brought into England must be carried either in English ships, or in ships from the country that was trading with England. Scottish merchants could only sell Scottish produce to England. Despite sharing a monarch, the Scots were actually being treated as foreign merchants by the English. This was popular with English merchants, but not with Scottish merchants. Other European countries were introducing similar laws to encourage the growth of their own fleets of merchant ships.

At the same time that Scotland's foreign trade was under attack, a series of dreadful harvests in the 1690s meant that famine became a fact of life for many Scots. In some areas of Scotland as many as one third of the population died of starvation and disease. Across the country, possibly twenty per cent of the population either died or moved away.

The Company of Scotland, trading to Africa and the Indies, was set up in 1695 to establish Scottish colonies. Its best known project was to establish a Scottish settlement at Darien, in Spanish-controlled Central America. The plan was to establish a shorter trade route between the Atlantic and Pacific Oceans, using the Scottish colony as a trading post. Goods could be exchanged, and merchants could avoid the long and dangerous sea voyage around the southern tip of South America. The colony was to be in what is Panama, today. This country now has a canal that links both oceans, constructed at the beginning of the twentieth century.

Source A

Summers and winters were so cold and barren that the cattle, flying fowls and insects all decayed. Our harvests did not take place in ordinary months, and many were sheep shearing in November. Many died, or lost the use of their feet and hands, working in frost and snow. Oatmeal became so scarce that it was expensive and many could not get it. I have seen women clapping their hand and tearing their clothes and crying, 'How shall we go home and see our children die of hunger?'.

From a book written by the Reverend Patrick Walker in the 1690s. He believed that the terrible problems facing Scotland may have been a punishment from God.

The first expedition sets sail, 1698

At first, many people in England were attracted to the Company of Scotland's plan. They hoped to buy shares in the company and make large profits. However, the powerful East India Company in England, which had been set up to develop trading links with India, was alarmed at the prospect of competition from a Scottish rival. The East India Company was able to put pressure on the English government, which told English investors not to put money into the Scottish company.

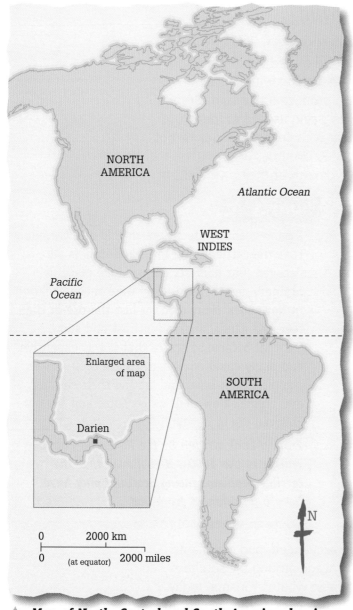

▲ *Map of North, Central and South America showing the location of the Darien colony.*

── *William Paterson*

The company's plan had been drawn up by William Paterson. He had been born in Scotland, but had made his fortune in England. He had been involved in the setting up of the Bank of England, and had become one of its first directors. Many Scottish merchants, lairds and burgesses invested large sums of money in the company. They believed that they would make a fortune from the Scottish colony. This was because they trusted Paterson, and believed that with his knowledge and expertise, the scheme could not fail. In turn, Paterson was prepared to set sail with the first expedition, accompanied by his wife and son.

Source B

◀ *The arms of the Company of Scotland.*

The first expedition to establish the colony set out in July 1698. There were three large ships: the *St Andrew*; the *Unicorn*; and the *Caledonia*. Also, there were two smaller ships: the *Endeavour* and the *Dolphin*. The ships carried 1200 passengers determined to start new lives in the colony. Within days of setting sail, the ships' captains realised that they had insufficient stores for the long voyage. They would have to purchase more stores at Madeira, an island in the Atlantic Ocean. This was a clear sign that the expedition was not as well planned as the colonists and shareholders might have expected. By the end of September 1698, the ships had reached the Caribbean. English colonies in this region had been ordered not to help the Scottish colonists, who finally reached Darien by the middle of October.

Questions

1. Why were Scottish merchants finding it more difficult to trade with England, and other European countries?

2. What do you think were the main causes of poverty and famine in Scotland in the 1690s?

3. Read Source A. Write down four problems facing Scottish farmers in the 1690s.

4. Why do you think that the Rev. Walker mentions the high price of oatmeal?
   (Clue: think of Scots and porridge oats)

5. How can you tell from the source that the Rev. Walker lived in Scotland in the 1690s?

6. How did the Company of Scotland hope to solve Scotland's economic problems?

7. Why did the English not put money into the Scottish plans for the colony in Panama?

8. Why was William Paterson important to the success or failure of the Company of Scotland's plans? Give at least two reasons for your answer.

Life in the Darien colony

Disaster!

The colonists drew maps of the area, and built a small settlement that they called New Edinburgh. This town was to be protected by Fort St Andrew. Unlike the Scottish towns that gave these new towns their names, the sites in Darien had a humid, tropical climate. Inland, there was jungle and swamps, and tropical insects like mosquitoes attacked the Scottish colonists. Many of the colonists developed fevers as a result of this unfortunate climate, and many died, including Paterson's wife and son.

The following July, in 1699, about 900 survivors from the first expedition abandoned the colony. They sailed north, towards New York. The group's morale had been weakened by disputes and arguments amongst themselves. Grief caused by the large number of deaths from fever and other illnesses added to the colony's problems. The final straw appeared to be the threat of a Spanish attack.

Several hundred colonists died on the voyage north to New York. Only the ship *Caledonia* returned to Scotland. The plan had been for second and third expeditions to follow the first ships, and establish a large settlement. However, the colony had been abandoned before the second expedition set sail at the end of 1699. The ship carrying their food supply had caught fire, and a Spanish fleet had arrived to blockade the harbour at New Edinburgh. The colony was finally abandoned in March 1700.

The project was a total failure largely because of poor planning and preparation, but there were other reasons:

- Company directors helped themselves to much of the investors' money.
- The hostile climate was not suitable for a European colony.
- The Spanish were not prepared to allow the Scots to set up a colony.
- The decision of English merchants and bankers not to support the scheme made it unlikely that the colony would succeed.
- At the time, many Scots blamed William III's government for persuading the English not to support the Scottish scheme.

Questions

1. Why do you think the second expedition set off, when the first expedition had abandoned the Darien colony?

2. Discuss in small groups:

Why do you think that so many Scottish colonists died at Darien?

56

The Act of Union 1707

― Why was it difficult to find a royal heir to Queen Anne?

Queen Mary died in 1694, and her husband, William III, died in 1702. They had no children as heirs. Anne, Mary's sister, became queen. Anne was nearly forty when she came to the throne. She was married to Prince George of Denmark, and all of her children died before she became queen, so she had no son or daughter to succeed her.

The English Parliament insisted that the next ruler must be a Protestant member of the Stewart royal family. The English Act of Succession in 1701 said that only members of the Church of England could rule in that country. Anne's second cousin, Sophia, was selected (see family tree on page 31). She was married to a German, the Elector of Hanover. However, Anne outlived her cousin, so Sophia's son became George I on the death of Queen Anne, in 1714.

The Scottish Parliament was not happy with the choice of Sophia as heir to the throne, although most Scots did not want a Catholic Stewart to become their monarch either. At that time, there were at least 40 members of the Stewart family with a better claim than George to the Scottish and English thrones. Most were Catholics but some of them were Protestant.

― The Pretender

James VII had died in 1701, and his son claimed to be James VIII (see family tree on page 31). He was known as the Pretender, from the French word 'pretendre', meaning to claim, as he claimed at this time the thrones of Scotland, England and Ireland.

Source A

▶ *The Old Pretender, James Stewart.*

In 1702, the English were at war with France, fighting the War of the Spanish Succession that lasted until 1714. The French king, Louis XIV, was happy to support the Jacobites in order to cause trouble for his English enemies. The 'Auld Alliance' (see page 5) was at work again. However, England wanted to make sure of Scottish support in their fight against France by uniting the two countries. The Scots, therefore, thought that they were in a strong position to choose the heir to Queen Anne.

By 1704, the Scottish Parliament had passed two new laws that displeased the English government. The 'Act anent Peace and War' (1703) made it clear that the Scots wanted to have their own foreign policy, and decide whether they would make peace or go to war whenever their priorities were not the same as the English. The Act of Security in 1704 made it clear that the Scots were not prepared to accept Sophia as heir to the Scottish throne without a struggle. Also, the Scots refused to give Anne's government any money to fight the French unless the English government recognised Scottish independence in these matters.

Questions

1. Why do you think that the Scots were unhappy with the English choice of a successor for Queen Anne?

2. In what way were the Jacobites pro-French?

3. What made the Scots think that they could force the English into doing what the Scots wanted?

Worsening relations: The 'Worcester Affair'

A clear sign that relations between both countries were deteriorating was the 'Worcester Affair'. In August 1704, an English ship, the Worcester, sailed into the Scottish harbour of Fraserburgh carrying a valuable cargo. The Scots allowed its captain to sail south to the Firth of Forth, then seized the ship. The Scots accused its captain and crew of piracy. They claimed that Captain Thomas Green had been involved in the disappearance of two Company of Scotland ships, the Speedy Return and the Content. Despite having no real evidence, Captain Green and two of his crew were hanged for piracy at Leith.

The English reacted to this Scottish hostility by passing the Alien Act in 1705. This English law said that Scots were aliens or foreigners, the same as any other nationality. As a result, there would be no trade between England and Scotland until the Scots agreed to Princess Sophia being recognised as the heir to the Scottish throne. The threat of a trade war between Scotland and its more wealthy neighbour forced many Scots to reconsider their attitude to union with England. Scotland could not afford to lose what little trade they had with England.

The steps to Union

The Treaty of Union was negotiated in 1706. There had been much discussion in 1705 over whether the union should be a 'federal' or an 'incorporating' union of Scotland and England.

- A federal union would mean closer links between the governments of both countries. The monarch, and the king or queen's representatives, would have a great deal of influence over government policy in Scotland, but there would still be a Scottish Parliament. Also, the Scots would send MPs to a British Parliament that dealt with the most important matters, such as foreign trade and national defence.

- An incorporating union would mean that the Scottish Parliament, with its 247 members, would disappear. The number of representatives from Scotland's nobility, shires and burghs would be much smaller in any British parliament. On the other hand, elections to the Scottish Parliament were rare; only one new parliament was elected between 1689 and 1707. In future, Scottish laws would be made by the British Parliament at Westminster. How Scotland was governed in its shires and burghs would not really change.

59

Union!

The idea of Scotland and England being united was not new. Edward I, King of England, had tried to conquer Scotland in the 1290s. Henry VIII's 'rough wooing' of Mary Queen of Scots, on behalf of his son, had also been an attempt to unite both kingdoms (see page 15). James VI had become James I of England, and he had continued to rule Scotland successfully from England (see pages 32–3). In the 1650s, Oliver Cromwell had used military force to unite Scotland and England, with a single British Parliament at Westminster (see page 42). For many Scots in the seventeenth century, Scottish independence was represented by having a Presbyterian Church of Scotland, rather than a parliament in Edinburgh.

Supporters of an 'incorporating' union believed that Scotland would be better off, and more secure, if it united with its English neighbour. Scottish merchants wanted to be able to trade on equal terms with countries in England's empire. The Scots who negotiated the treaty with England were willing to take bribes or gifts from the English government. However, they obtained a deal that brought many advantages to Scotland. Negotiating a good deal was made easier by the hostility of many ordinary Scots to the Union. The Union Treaty had to be seen to be in the best interests of the Scottish nation.

The Treaty of Union became law on 16 January 1707. The main points of the treaty are listed below and at the top of page 61.

- The Scots agreed to Princess Sophia becoming the heir to the thrones of both kingdoms.
- Scotland and England would be united into one kingdom called Great Britain.
- The United Kingdom of Great Britain and Ireland would have one Parliament. A new joint British Parliament would be elected in place of the separate English and Scottish Parliaments.
- Scottish merchants would be able to trade on equal terms in English ports and English colonies.
- A common United Kingdom flag would be designed.

60

Source B

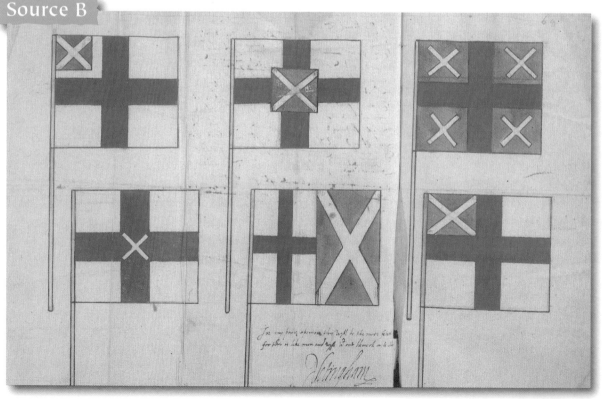

Designs for the union flag. ▲

- Currency, weights and measures, and so on, would be standardised, which meant that the English currency, and English weights and measures, had to be adopted in Scotland.
- The Scottish legal system would remain the same as before, but Scottish laws would be passed in the British Parliament.
- The Presbyterian Scottish Kirk would remain separate from the Episcopal Church of England.
- Scotland would send 16 Lords to the House of Lords in London, and 45 Members of Parliament (MPs) to the British Parliament at Westminster. (At Westminster, there were more than 200 Lords and 513 MPs).
- The Scots would agree to pay a share of the English government's debts; to pay new taxes on salt and malt for brewing beer; and the Company of Scotland would cease trading.
- Finally, the Scots would receive the sum of £398,000, known as the 'Equivalent'. This money would pay salary arrears owed to government officials in Scotland, and compensate the Scots for the loss of the Company of Scotland, as well as their having to share in England's national debt.

Source C

I was introduced to Mr Cole, a ninety-four-year old who retained all of his mental faculties. He told me that he had a distinct recollection of seeing the wagons sent to Scotland with the Equivalent money ... guarded by a troop of Dragoons (soldiers, riding on horseback). It was followed by an immense multitude (crowd) hissing and swearing at their leaders for giving in to their ancient and most long-lasting enemy, with such a costly bribe ...

An extract describing the 'Equivalent' from the autobiography of Thomas Somerville, who was born in 1714.

Many people in Scotland reacted angrily to the Union, and riots and demonstrations took place. However, throughout these negotiations, the opponents of an 'incorporating' union were disorganised and lacked any sense of unity. Only those who were members of the Scottish Parliament could vote for or against the treaty proposals. The Country Party which opposed the Union was made up of:

- some Jacobites
- nobles who had fallen out with the leaders of the successful Court party, that supported an incorporating union
- Presbyterians, worried about union with Anglican England and its bishops
- Episcopalians, worried about the English accepting a Presbyterian Church of Scotland
- investors in the Company of Scotland who wanted to negotiate generous compensation from England for the failure of the Darien scheme (see Chapter 10)
- supporters of a federal union.

Questions

1. The execution of Captain Green and two of his crew was a disgraceful event. Why do you think that so many Scots wanted these men to be executed?

2. What differences would an incorporating union make to the way that Scotland was governed?

3. Had Scotland and England ever been united before 1707?

4. Describe the main points of the Treaty of Union that:

  a. affected both countries
  b. affected Scotland.

5. Read Source C on page 61.

  a. What does Mr Cole say the attitude of most Scots to the payment of the Equivalent money was?
  b. Why is Mr Cole a useful source of information about how Scots reacted to the 'Equivalent' being sent north by the English?
  c. Why would it be useful to know when Thomas Somerville met Mr Cole?

Extended writing

1. Why did the Scottish Parliament agree to the Treaty of Union with England?

Consider:

- the main political problems facing the Scots between 1690 and 1707 (e.g. who should succeed Queen Anne; the Jacobites who supported the Pretender)
- the main economic problems that faced the Scots at that time (e.g. the failure of the Darien scheme)
- why Scottish opposition to the treaty was not very effective
- why the English wanted to unite with the Scots
- whether or not the money paid to those Scots who voted for the Treaty of Union made much difference to the course of events?

In conclusion, decide what you think were the one or two most important reasons why the Scottish Parliament agreed to the Union.

12 *The transatlantic slave trade*

The Union of 1707 enabled Scots to play a part in the development of what had been England's, and now were Britain's, colonies and trading factories. Scottish merchants, farmers, craftsmen, sailors and soldiers could take advantage of the opportunities provided by overseas trade. This included the slave trade.

The origins of the slave trade

Slavery is the ownership and forced labour of captives or prisoners. Slaves can be bought and sold, and in many societies the children of slaves automatically become slaves too. After the defeat of the Moors in Spain and Portugal in the fifteenth century, captured Muslims were used as slaves by the victorious Christians. Soon, these prisoners of war were joined by slaves imported from Africa. A regular trade in slaves was established between Spain and Portugal, and the Guinea coast of Africa.

Europeans growing sugar cane on Atlantic islands, such as Madeira and the Canaries, used a mixture of slave and free labour to work on their farms or plantations. In the sixteenth century, African slaves were transported to European colonies in the Americas. This was the beginning of the transatlantic slave trade that would transform West Africa, and play a huge part in the history of Western Europe and the Americas.

The transatlantic slave trade grew quickly in the sixteenth century, as European countries set up colonies in South and Central America. Where conditions were suitable, the Spanish and Portuguese grew sugar cane to be processed and shipped back to Europe. Sugar plantations were established in Brazil, Mexico, Paraguay, the Pacific coast of South America, and islands in the Caribbean.

The Europeans required a large labour force but they found the native inhabitants either unwilling or unable to work on their plantations. Few Europeans were willing to sail across the Atlantic and work on sugar plantations. Therefore, the Spanish and Portuguese shipped thousands of African captives across the Atlantic to work in their colonies. Next, the Dutch used their enormous shipping resources to supply the slave ships required to transport tens of thousands of Africans to the New World.

England and the slave trade

Early in the seventeenth century, the English took over Barbados, Jamaica and several other Caribbean islands, while the French settled in Guadaloupe and Martinique. European governments were attracted to the wealth that would come from owning colonies in the New World, and from the crops grown (using slave labour), such as sugar, tobacco and rice, which could then be shipped back to Europe.

The transatlantic slave trade was a complicated network of businesses and trading agreements, but merchants, shipowners, traders and business men established a 'triangular trade' (see map on page 64).

- Alcohol, weapons, and textiles were shipped from Europe to Africa, to be traded for captives in Africa.

- Then African slaves would be shipped to South America or the Caribbean on the 'Middle Passage', where they would be exchanged for sugar, rice, tobacco and, later, raw cotton.

- These products were then taken back and sold for large profits in Europe.

In reality, the trade was much more complex than this simple description. By the eighteenth century, two out of five slave ships sailed to Africa from colonies in South America, rather than from Europe.

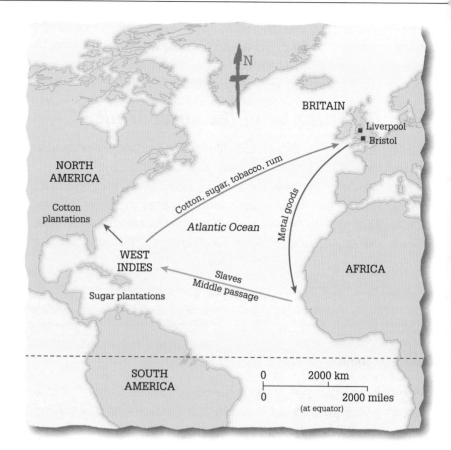

The 'triangular trade'. ▲

The 'Tobacco Lords'

When the Union was agreed in 1707, Scottish merchants were able to enjoy the profits of trade with what had become Britain's colonies. Scottish merchants traded with colonies in North America and the Caribbean. The North American plantations produced tobacco, and the Jamaican plantations grew and processed sugar cane into its many products. The port of Glasgow on Scotland's west coast, together with other towns along the Firth of Clyde, made large profits from colonial trade. They supplied the rest of Britain, and much of Europe, with colonial produce.

The wealthy merchants of Glasgow became known as 'Tobacco Lords'. They purchased large estates and plantations in the Americas, and employed Scottish emigrants in every position, from estate agents and managers, to slave drivers and overseers.

Questions

1. Why did Europeans decide to transport African captives to the Americas as slave labour?

2. Why is the term 'triangular trade' used to describe the trade between Europe, Africa and the American colonies?

3. Why do you think Glasgow's merchants became known as 'Tobacco Lords'?